Alias Rich

Nanette
Ackerman

Alias Richard Lee

Pictures of a Chaplin actor

(Based on the memoirs of Marguerite Ackerman)

Nanette Ackerman

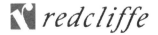 redcliffe

First published in 2011 by Redcliffe Press Ltd.,
81g Pembroke Road, Bristol BS8 3EA

www.redcliffepress.co.uk
e: info@redcliffepress.co.uk

ISBN 978-1-908326-04-1

British Library Cataloguing-in-Publication Data
A catalogue record for this book is available from the British
Library

Set in 12/14pt Minion

Cover design by Mark Cavanagh
Design and typesetting by Harper Phototypesetters Ltd.
Printed by MPG Books, Bodmin, Cornwall

Contents

Introduction

Not so long ago, I was flicking through the pages of a bargain book when I was struck by the photograph of a very familiar – though thickly made-up – face. The book was *My Life in Pictures*, by Charlie Chaplin. The face was not Chaplin's. It belonged to one of his side-kicks. At once a story that I had unearthed a few years before came flooding back.

Charlie Chaplin is the focus of attention in his films. Even when I am scanning a reel for my own purpose, I find my eye constantly drawn towards this ingenious performer and his pantomime. It is little wonder that a certain supporting actor in the background escapes notice. Richard Percy Berry, alias Richard Lee, was ever the escapologist. He escaped the Law, he escaped the bloody battle fields of World War One and the wife who loved him until the day she died. No doubt this adventurer escaped the consequences of others of his actions during his years in self-imposed exile from England. But it is time to pin him down: through the memoirs of the beautiful wife he left behind, the testimonies of his children and through the mute photographs that say so much which were pasted into a scrapbook in times gone by. The story begins over a hundred years ago.

Beginnings

It is easy for a romantic spirit to drift back into the past. Yet I often wondered why things seem so much brighter in retrospect. The answer is this: when we travel into the past or fast-forward into the future, we are engaging the spirit and are not bound by the pains and strictures of the moment. We may glance over our shoulders wistfully, but something of the raw pain has gone. So as I begin once more to trace the lives of my grandparents, celebrating each rich jewel that I unearth, I feel that I must take care not to ride rough-shod over their story. These people experienced their *present*; the sweat, the tears, the anguishes of their daily lives. It would be the easiest thing in the world to blame my grandfather for the pain he caused. But I haven't peeped into every corner of their lives, experiencing every bounding pulse and facial tic like an omniscient novelist. Even if I had, who am I to judge? So why do I tell the story? It is history, and it asks to be told.

In 1967, there was a fire in a Devon nursing home. Letters tied up in a blue ribbon perished in the blaze. The letters were sent from an actor, Richard Lee, to his beautiful wife who he promised to send for when the time was right. She waited patiently for over twenty years, but the wanderer never returned and he never sent for her. I watch, in my mind's eye, the edges of the letters brown and curl, the licking flames feasting on fairy tales.

This is a story of a grandfather who died far away in San Francisco many years before I was born. There are times that his life unrolls before me like a series of broken images, the dramatic trailer of a film. These tantalising moments are bridged by my dreams and by the wraiths of times past. Yet for all the incertitude and Chinese whispers, there is much evidence to give truth to this account, some of it in pictures.

It is over thirty years since the story of how Richard Lee left my grandmother to appear in the early Chaplin films disturbed my sleep and occupied most of my waking hours. Yet, for me, the story begins long before that. It begins with the discovery of a faded photograph of him in an old scrapbook belonging to my grandmother. The setting is the Salt Box, a tiny cottage on the edge of a Cornish moor. I was only fifteen years old, but I still remember the essence of conversation.

"Gosh, you were so beautiful," I said. My grandmother didn't reply. Then I discovered a small strip of photographs wedged into the crease of the book. I withdrew it and studied it. "Who's he?" There was a long pause as she pretended to be busy. "He was your grandfather, and he was an actor – in Chaplin films," she said at last.

The edgy reply was the end of the conversation and there was uneasiness as I continued to turn the pages. My grandmother may have been reticent about the past, but my father told me, in florid detail, much about his parents as time went by and a colourful story began to unfold.

In 1980, my thoughts turned again to the old scrapbook. I borrowed it and turned the pages with my father. Many times he reminisced about being released from terrible foster homes and moving to the Cornish coast. He was a writer and a natural story-teller. The way he talked about his unfortunate childhood was moving and very compelling. I was hungry for every detail and began to detach myself from the realities of the present and dwell longer and longer in the imagined past. I was obsessed with the story of my grandparents, and felt deeply for the two infants whose father had left them and their mother so brutally on a cold February morning in 1909.

Important questions remained. Why did Richard leave the country so abruptly and what was he up to in those early years? And why did Marguerite leave her infants in the hands of disreputable foster parents for much of their childhoods? These were questions answered in part by the old photographs, and in part by family whispers still bound long ago in time. What is more, some of the clouded answers were given to me in a series of strange dreams in which I glided back into the past. It was then that Marguerite's memoirs came to light, secretly written in shorthand. The story begins with Richard and Marguerite's early lives.

Dick and Daisy

Richard Percy Berry was born in 1885. He was the son of a drayman who came from a farming family. They moved to London in early Edwardian times and settled in Victoria. From what I gathered from my father, Richard's mother disliked books. She made it clear that she had no time for literature and that she only respected work of the "pick and shovel" variety. She spent much of her time scrubbing things which needn't be scrubbed, her face carved in stone. Bearing in mind the stifling atmosphere in which he grew up, it is little wonder that Richard turned his attention to the theatre and chanced his luck as an actor.

A picture from the scrapbook shows Richard on the stage at the wheel of a dummy car. I did some detective work. It could be a scene from George Bernard Shaw's *Man and Superman* which was written in 1903. Things have since taken an ironic twist, for the play is about a Byronic anti-hero like Don Juan, who is pursued by women. Richard looks very young in the picture, and from the costume that he wears: sharply creased trousers cut to the ankle with no turn-ups and a three quarters overcoat – a rough date would be 1905, slightly before or after he met Marguerite.[1] I assume it was a provincial production, and the backdrop resembles Edinburgh.

Richard, possibly in 'Man and Superman', by George Bernard Shaw, c.1905

He was working as an office boy in the Haymarket Theatre either at the time he met Marguerite or after he married her. Whatever the case, it would have rankled to have his activities in the theatre curtailed and no doubt he resented being tied down. Added to this, for Richard, there would have been some feeling of inadequacy in the presence of Marguerite's family. In an age of class distinction, they felt that he lacked gentility and was by no means good enough for Marguerite. Arthur, Marguerite's brother, certainly did not like him. Richard had neither the family's education nor their musical and theatrical background. To be fair to her mother, Anne Ackerman, once they were married she helped all she could, but from

[1] London: Methuen, 1979 *A History of English Costume* by Iris Brooke.

the outset she harboured suspicions and at best found her son-in-law unreliable.

Marguerite Ackerman was born in 1886 and grew up in Belgravia, London, the daughter of the celebrated opera singer, Charles Ackerman, who had sung at the coronation of King Edward the Seventh and partnered Dame Clara Butt. Her brother, Arthur, a chorister at Chapel Royal, also sang at the coronation and was later to become soloist to King George the Fifth. Marguerite had a quick wit but was educated at home where she studied music, played the piano and read poetry. She was an expressive, though melo-dramatic soul who always read beautifully and dreamed of becoming an actress "just like Ellen Terry".[2] With the accession to the throne of Edward the Seventh, women now enjoyed a finer status on the stage, and Marguerite would have benefited from all the necessary contacts in the profes-sional theatre – had the time been right. Her childhood had been one of music and laughter and comparative luxury with a small complement of servants.

In 1903, tragedy struck the family. Charles Ackerman died of pneumonia on board ship as he returned from a successful operatic tour of America, and he was buried ceremoniously at sea. It was a terrible shock and quite unexpected. Moreover, the family had been completely dependent on his earnings. It gradually sank in that they were running out of money and the servants were asked to leave. Anne Ackerman, who had been an actress before her marriage, found work at the Theatre Royal, Haymarket. Dorothy, the serious academic of the family, who dreamed of being a lion tamer, was given a place at a Masonic boarding school and later won a scholarship to Girton College, Cambridge. Arthur left Chapel Royal soon

---

[2] The famous daughter of Victorian actor, Fred Terry.

ACKERMAN & WYNNE

In Folk Songs, Operatic and other Duets.

From the Stoll, Syndicate, and Principal London and Provincial Variety and Concert Halls.

ARTHUR ACKERMAN.

Son of the late famous Baritone, Charles Ackerman, of Westminster Abbey and the Westminster Singers. He has studied music in most of its branches, commencing at the age of five under his father, and later under Sir Frederick Bridge and Dr. Alcock.

As a boy, was soloist in the choir of H.M. Chapels Royal, St. James' Palace, where he had the honour of appearing before Their Majesties the King and Queen, on one occasion being presented with a brooch by Queen Alexandra.

In 1902, he sang at the Coronation of King Edward and Queen Alexandra in Westminster Abbey, the choir on this occasion consisting of the pick of the world's most famous singers.

Mr. Ackerman is a well-known exponent of English Church music, Oratorio, Folk Songs and traditional music, and many of the Folk Songs he sings with Miss Wynne have been collected and arranged by him, the best known being: "Drink to me only with thine eyes," and "Sally in our Alley."

He has successfully fulfilled engagements at the following London Theatres:—The Haymarket, The Criterion, The Garrick, His Majesty's, The St. James', and The Prince of Wales', and has also played the Stoll, Moss, L.T.V., and Syndicate Tours.

JENNY WYNNE.

A young Contralto who has quickly taken a place amongst the best Artistes of the day.

She has appeared with remarkable success at The Royal Albert Hall, The Queen's Hall, and the principal London and Provincial Ballad and Orchestral Concerts, in company with many of the world's Star Artistes.

She is the possessor of a true contralto voice of wonderful range, which is at the same time rich and mellow in quality.

Added to her many gifts she has a great personality, and the London Press has predicted a fine career for her.

afterwards with a monetary gift from King George the Fifth, and forged a successful stage career. It left Marguerite being given the sober advice to train as a secretary in case she should (prophetically) fall on hard times.

It was now that Frederick, a chorister from Chapel Royal, declared his love for Charles Ackerman's beautiful daughter. He turned her head, but he was to be disappointed when the "fascinating" would-be actor Richard Berry came onto the scene. It was a long while before Freddie accepted defeat.

A few weeks before the memoirs were discovered, I asked my father about Marguerite's girlhood and wondered what she was doing at the time she met Richard. He did not know much about her early years although there was plenty of hearsay. He had vague recollections of her being on the stage – that was all. I was dissatisfied and continued to try to piece together a picture of my grandparents' first meeting.

Perhaps they were already acquainted when they met in St. James's Park. It was a favourite place of my grandmother's. They were bound to discuss the theatre. They had this in common. I have always believed that daydreams have surprising powers so, in the absence of solid information, I shall allow myself to dream.

My story begins as old sepia photographs at once come alive and give way to a palette of gentle pastels. In my imagination it is a lazy Edwardian summer and the last of the May blossoms are just fluttering onto the ground. I come to land on the edge of a small but busy lake, where couples are strolling arm-in-arm and nannies wheel perambulators. A handful of people are feeding the ducks, others are symbolically sailing boats across to the other side.

A beautiful woman, wearing a white dress, half turns. She stops feeding the ducks and opens her parasol – to frame her face rather than to shield herself from the sun. She looks right through me and smiles uncertainly at the handsome young man nearby as he raises his boater hat. It is strange to witness vibrant flesh upon bones long turned to dust, but somehow I am invited to listen to their conversation. The young man casts his eye over the lady-like figure standing before him and applies charm:

"Good afternoon."

"Good afternoon."

"It's Miss Ackerman, isn't it? You know, you shouldn't feed the ducks?"

"I certainly shall," she replies, with her nose in the air, continuing to feed the ducks.

He laughs: "Dear, oh, dear! Do you always play the wilful lady?"

"I beg your pardon? I *am* a lady." She scrutinises him with a sense of vague recognition. "Do I know you?"

"I hope so. Richard. Dick Berry. We met at the Haymarket."

Richard is slightly built, but he has a fascinating face supported by an easy and attractive way of moving. Marguerite could well imagine him on the stage. She has a tremendous love for the theatre and finds him quite disarming, although she will not show it. She is conscious of keeping her distance. After all, it was clear that Richard was not a gentleman like Chapel Royal Frederick and her other suitors – and he had a roguish twinkle in his eye.

"Ah, yes, the aspiring actor. You were going to be a *famous* actor, were you not?"

"Well . . . I hope to get lucky. I've had a few parts. I'm up for *Man and Superman* . . ."

"The Shaw?

"Yep."

"I've read it. It's about the adventurer. It's rather modern and naturalistic, isn't it? Have you read it?"

"Not yet. No, haven't had the chance."

"Oh, but you must. What plays do you like? I absolutely adore Shakespeare."

Richard is not a literary man, so he changes the subject. "Look, shall we sit down – over here?"

"Yes, I should like that."

"You know, you're much more beautiful than Ellen Terry."

"Oh, really? But she is an accomplished actress."

"But she hasn't the fire in her eyes . . ."

At this, Marguerite rises and takes a step away, but there is still a discernible interest in her conversation. She is attracted to his penitence.

"Sorry, it was forward of me."

"Yes, very forward," she admonishes.

"Well, Miss Ackerman . . ."

"Marguerite."

"Yes, alright, Daisy," he laughs.

She plays with him now: "Only members of my immediate family call me Daisy."

"Well Dais, then. And where is your immediate family?"

"We live in Belgravia."

"Yes, I remember now. Lucky Belgravia. We're in Victoria. Not too far away, you can walk it from here, so I s'pose we're neighbours."

"Yes, I suppose we are."

He withdraws his pocket watch. "Damn, I've got to go. I'll look out for you again then, Dais."

"Marguerite."

"Perhaps we could have tea at the Haymarket?"

"Perhaps," she says as she pauses for effect and frames her face with the parasol, "or perhaps not. However, I shall be here tomorrow. You know, I always feed the ducks."

She had a way of tossing her head disdainfully, even in old age. Perhaps she did so then. He had surely called her beautiful, after all he was a charmer and she was beautiful. And no doubt those (or similar) words re-echoed in her heart: "You're much more beautiful than Ellen Terry . . . She hasn't the fire in her eyes . . ."

So much for an imagined conversation, but I believe I am near the mark. The truth is that Marguerite fell head-over-heels in love with Richard. I discovered her 1905 verses to him pasted to a page in the old scrapbook. They evoke her feelings during those early months.

To Richard

All the earth must seem more fair,
　　Nature's beauty, not so rare, beside you.
Sunshine glinting in your hair,
　　All the glory lingers there, beside you.

Nightingale's enchanted note
　　Trilling from his magic throat, adoring.
Singing zephyrs gently float
　　Whispering of things remote, imploring!

So when I am from your side,
　　I can never hope to hide my longing.
And my thoughts at eventide,
　　O'er the moonlit spaces wide, go thronging.

In your eyes I long to see
　　Love enshrined, and I would be beside you.
Oh, the joy to ever be
　　Loving deep and tenderly beside you!

Their courtship was brief. Documentation, dated 1906, showed that their first child, Phyllis, was conceived out of wedlock. They were forced to get married, and soon afterwards moved away from central London to Surbiton in Surrey. Holly Villa was a much smaller house than the one in which she grew up, but Marguerite was besotted with Richard and nothing else mattered.

Despite an unsteady start to their marriage, Marguerite (whom Richard called Daisy) still adored her husband. It was said that, after her second child was born in 1908, all she wanted was for them to be together, to live for each other. My grandmother had many virtues, but, if she had a character flaw, it was possessiveness. She loved Richard too much, while his redeeming factor was that, at twenty, he had been much too young to be tied down. After the initial passion had died away, Richard no doubt felt trapped and somewhat stifled by outpourings of affection coupled with the responsibility of marriage. His wife could not hope to live wrapped around with love indefinitely. Moreover, Richard could never give her the kind of life to which she had been accustomed. He changed. Occasions like my imagined sunny day in St. James's Park soon turned to snow, and snow to slush. In the New Year of 1909, things went from bad to worse, as my grandmother's secret memoirs testify.

Richard and Marguerite, c.1908

Marriage

I shall take up her pen for a while and let her tell the original story. The short-hand text had been locked in an exercise book and stowed away on a shelf to gather dust with her old scrapbook. It was odd and strangely thrilling when the story was deciphered, opening a door into the past. She writes in the third person.

"It had been said that Marguerite and her boy lover had married impulsively far too soon. Heads were shaken at the wonder of their action, but they were both quite used to having their own way, and quite overruled opposition. For the first year or so they were ideally and wholly happy. Their bliss was well and truly doubled when their first child, Phyllis was born. She was their pride and joy, and of course, the prettiest and most wonderful baby in the entire universe. To Marguerite the baby was all absorbing, and all day she devoted most of her time and interest to the little girl. She neglected many of her household duties, and, sometimes herself, to pet and play with the baby. At that time Richard never grumbled. He was away at business all day in the city. When he arrived home at night the baby was in bed, and Marguerite was free to lavish him with all her attentions and love. His nature was warm and affectionate, and in return she needed affection too. She was never so happy as when she had her loved ones with her.

"When little Phyllis was nearly two, another baby was expected. Marguerite was deeply depressed. [Her depression is evident from a photograph taken at the time]. For some time now, things had not been going well for herself and Richard. Their means were small, and with increased expenses, they began to find it very difficult to manage. Richard worked late in the office to earn extra money, and when he arrived home he was tired, sometimes discouraged. Despite her own depression, Marguerite did her best to keep him cheerful, but she found it a struggle all the way round. Sometimes she even wondered whether they had done the right thing marrying so young. After all, Richard was still only a boy, and it didn't seem fair that he should be so overburdened with responsibility. Marguerite felt guilty that she had not stopped to consider that aspect in the rush of passion that had swept them into marriage. Life was hard, it seemed, and couldn't be all love and kisses as she had hoped. One still had to live, eat, be housed and clothed. And now there would be an additional member of the family to be considered.

"One day, when Marguerite was feeling particularly tired and depressed, her mother paid her a visit. Anne Ackerman was shocked at her daughter's appearance, and told her she had let herself go and needed looking after, and that she ought not to be left alone all day. She decided to wait until Richard came home. When he arrived, she insisted to the already worried man, that Marguerite needed to be taken special care of until the baby was born. This Richard already knew, yet realised that he couldn't offer a solution to the problem. After all, he needed to work, and couldn't afford domestic help at that time. He said he wished he could do more for Daisy, and realised that he could not give her anything like the life she had been used to. "So there it is," he concluded.

"On her arrival home, Anne talked to other members of the family about ways and means of helping the two young people. At first it was suggested that she should go to stay at the little house in Surbiton until Marguerite had her baby. However, the idea was dismissed as inconvenient because Anne had her work at the Haymarket to consider. Then suddenly she remembered the top flat, converted for income after Charles Ackerman's death, was soon to become vacant. This consisted of two rooms and a small kitchen, and the tenants were expected to be moving out the following week. Plans made, Anne Ackerman wrote a letter and posted it off to Surbiton immediately.

"The next morning a letter arrived at Holly Villa. Marguerite tore open the envelope impatiently, and called to Richard who was busy shaving. She rushed upstairs clutching the letter in her hand and entered the bathroom. They were both puzzled. Richard leaned over Marguerite's shoulder as she read aloud.

139, Cambridge Street,
London, W1.

My Dearest Children,
 The Browns are moving out of the top flat here next week, and I was wondering whether it would be more convenient for you to come and live in Town just now. The rent of the flat is not high, and in any case, Richard would save on fares. The rest of the family would like you to be near us, and it would not be quite so lonely for you, Marguerite.

Let me know as soon as possible my dears. I do hope you will decide to come.

With love from all the family,

Your affectionate Mother."

The humid bathroom in the tiny terraced house begins to shape in my mind. Richard has paused to listen. Now, in the half-steam, he continues scraping a path with a cut-throat razor through the soap suds across his dimpled cheek. He wipes the razor and looks at his wife. There is a scent of soap for a moment in this colourful parallel universe of mine. Evidently, my grandmother suffered a twinge of anxiety. She continues:

"Marguerite looked up at Richard pleadingly. She was excited at the prospect of being back at the big house. But Richard remained doubtful, and it was not until she explained how much better it would be for her to have some company now that the baby was due at any time, that he finally condescended. With everything agreed upon, Richard advised Marguerite to reply to the letter post haste. For the moment, 'little Daisy', as he often called her, was so happy, that she called him her precious beloved and kissed his soapy chin. With new-found elation, she went downstairs to carry on with the interrupted breakfast preparations.

"At the end of the month, the young ones found themselves in Belgravia again, and were safely installed in the top flat. It was good for Marguerite to be back in the lovely home where she had grown up, and things seemed to improve for a while, every-day tensions eased. Richard certainly found it useful only to have a short ride to the office, instead of a tiresome journey by train, followed by another tedious ride by omnibus. And all day long, Marguerite was petted and fussed. She was made to rest while elderly aunts took Phyllis out for walks. She certainly benefited from these attentions.

"Then one night, Richard came home very late. Marguerite had at last gone to bed, after anxiously awaiting his return. Eventually, after what seemed like an interminable night of sheer loneliness, Marguerite heard Richard's footsteps as he made his way upstairs. He peeped round the door to his sad little wife. He was apologetic, and Marguerite was relieved when he gave an explanation of 'Just a little party with the boys.' He assured her that he was quite unable to get out of it. He kissed her sorrowful face and begged her to forgive him. He was so penitent and at the same time so affectionate, that Marguerite took him to her heart and loved him even more.

"But a few nights later, Marguerite felt so benumbed. The same thing had happened. Once more she had lain awake feeling anxious, lonely, listening to the monotonous sound of the carriage clock as it ticked away the minutes and subsequently the lonely hours. When eventually Richard did arrive home it was near dawn. This time he was not so penitent, or so pleasant, moreover he smelt of spirits. At this Marguerite froze with fear. Oh, no, not her Richard, she thought. Someone must have played a trick on him by giving him whisky. Richard was soon asleep, but, much distressed, Marguerite continued to lie awake. Her mind was full of unpleasant notions, and repeatedly she asked the same questions. Why did Richard want to stay out all night with the boys, when she and little Phyllis were at home waiting for him? Didn't he understand how much she needed him, even more now? Every few moments a smattering of reassurance would creep in to calm her mind. But of course, she told herself, Richard loved her as much as ever. Perhaps he needed a little relaxation after his long working day. Everything would be all right after she had had the baby, and was her old self again. Her aunts could mind the sleeping babies, and she could go out with Richard occasionally. He wouldn't want 'the boys' when he had his wife to take out.

"For the next week or so, she tried not to worry too much when the nights became more frequent. She consoled herself that everything would change for the better when the baby was born. It was due any time now, a boy, she hoped. Richard wanted a son, and she thought that if only she could give him one all would be well."

Despair

"Christmas came and went; a time much revelled in by Richard, who continued his misconduct. Marguerite hadn't enjoyed her Christmas like she usually did. She felt particularly low-spirited, and thought that the baby would never arrive, until . . .

"It was a snowy night, the day after Boxing Day, when the nurse and doctor were fetched. The sky was over-filled with a magical glow, releasing the flakes thickly and swiftly through the night air. They settled gracefully on chimney pots and rooftops in the quiet backwaters of Old London Town. It was during the snowstorm that a little baby was born. Happily, Marguerite exhibited the perfect baby boy to his proud father. She would call him Charles Ackerman, after her own, late famous father: Charles Ackerman Berry.

"In due time baby Charles was shown off to his doubting sister, Phyllis, who was now a toddler of nineteen months. At first she was jealous, and didn't like the idea of her mother cuddling another baby. But Phyllis was a philosophical child, and soon accepted the idea as something that had to be. It wasn't long before the little girl became so thrilled with her baby brother, that he was the idol of her heart.

"During the next week or so, Marguerite didn't see much of her husband. Of course he made regular visits to see the baby, but was not allowed to disturb her at night. He was sleeping somewhere downstairs, where the aunts were taking care of him. Yet Marguerite was contented, and made good progress towards recovering her usual health.

"When the baby was five weeks old, Marguerite once more began to do her house-keeping, with a little help from her two aunts, who were in their element with the little ones. While she rested in the afternoons, they gathered up the two babies, taking it in turns to push the perambulator around the block. Little Phyllis was led by the hand. She loved her 'Nanties', and enjoyed the daily excursions. Most of all she loved to ride with her brother when she was tired of walking.

"During the evening Marguerite continued to go to bed early, as the doctor had advised her to do until she was quite strong again. Richard was rarely home now, and usually had a meal with some of his many friends after leaving the office. He told Marguerite that in doing this, it would save her the trouble of preparing an evening meal for him. Contented with his (altogether phoney) thoughtfulness on those occasions, she usually had a little supper with the aunts. In fact, if it were not for the aunts and the two little ones to keep her busy, Marguerite would have been very lonely. (Anne Ackerman was rarely at home now, spending most of her time at the Haymarket).

"One night, very late, Marguerite was woken with a start. It was the sound of Richard stumbling into the bedroom. In a moment she sensed something was wrong. She switched on the light, which revealed Richard standing, with bent head, before the dressing table. Softly she called his name. He swayed lightly, but did not answer. Quickly she slipped out of bed and went to him. He told her, thickly, not to touch him, raising his hand to push her away. There was violence in the air. And then, in an agony of distress, she saw that he was holding a revolver! With a muffled sob, she flung her arms around his neck and kissed him. He smelt of spirits and was drunk. There was no doubt about his drunkenness. But the revolver, where did he get it, and why? Gently she led her husband to the crumpled bed. He sank into it, still with that sinister weapon clutched tightly in his right hand. Marguerite was positively fighting to hide her terror, and prayed silently to be guided by God. All of a-tremble she sat down beside Richard, putting her arms across his shoulders, caressingly. With a voice of persuasion she coaxed him into bed, telling him how tired he must be.

"Richard's speech continued to slur. Every so often he would utter that he was no darned good. With a flourish of the hand that still held the pistol, he indicated that he was going to end it all. With her heart beating almost aloud, Marguerite tried to reassure him. 'You're just over-tired,' she had said warmly, 'Come along, take your things off and have a sleep.' Cautiously she tried to undo his overcoat, but roughly he wrenched her out of the way, and got unsteadily onto his feet. Panic-stricken, she wondered whatever she was going to do. Was he going to kill them all? She shuddered at the thought of their two babies who were lying innocently asleep. She wanted to dash out of the room to protect them. She tried to talk him out of doing anything foolish; she begged him to tell her what the matter was, and asked if he was worried about anything in particular. 'Won't you tell Daisy all about it?' she implored. Richard only replied hoarsely that he was going to end it. 'Better end it, I'm no darned good.' By this time he was a weary, pathetic figure of a young man, who attracted pity rather than scorn. And the frightening-looking pistol still hung loosely in his right hand.

"Seeing that he was tired, Marguerite continued to coax him in between silent prayers of salvation. She begged him not to wake the sleeping babies, and said that everything would be sorted out in the morning. All Richard managed to utter in reply was 'No darn good to you, Daisy.'

"The long, formidable night was slowly dragging itself towards morning. Marguerite delved right down into herself, searching for the last little ounce of compassion and resilience. Now it was nearing dawn. She still found herself talking, persuading, anything to prevent him pulling the trigger and ending their lives for good. She tried to convince him how very much he meant to herself and their two babies. It wouldn't be long before she collapsed from sheer stress. She felt that all her strength was waning, and managed to croak exhaustedly, 'Be a dear, forget all this until the morning.'

"There was silence for a while, before Richard looked at her dully, his eyes roving around the room, expressionless-ly. Marguerite's prayers were answered. Suddenly aware of her opportunity, she took a firm grip on his arm, guiding him slowly and carefully towards the bed. 'Oh, God!' he breathed, and flung himself down, burying his face in the pillow. One arm was shrouding his head, the other, out-stretched over the eiderdown. All the while his fingers were jealously guarding the loosely-clasped revolver. With a certain amount of strength and new-found relief, Marguerite smoothed down his crumpled hair, murmuring soothingly, 'Poor old Richard, poor darling.' But still she was afraid to stir, just in case she roused him again. She was shivering, otherwise remaining silent, hoping and praying that he would fall asleep to enable her to remove the fearful looking gun and hide it. She noticed that he didn't move. At last he was asleep. She was trembling, and felt as though she was skating on thin ice as she reached across his hand, almost imperceptibly drawing the gun out of the way. She scarcely dared to move or breathe, as she tip-toed over to the chest-of-drawers. Wincing with every breath that she dared to take, she managed to open the drawer quite noiselessly, wedging the revolver deeply between some articles of clothing. There was still no sound from Richard, and not a sign that he missed the gun. She was convinced that by now he had at last fallen deeply asleep. She crept over towards the bed and gently removed his shoes, then quietly prised off his overcoat and jacket. She reached for her warm dressing gown and put it on. By now she was feeling miserably cold, having paid little attention to it before. Starting to shiver again, she crept into bed, switched off the light and snuggled down.

"But sleep was far away, and Marguerite felt wide awake. Now that the ordeal was over, she began to tremble uncontrollably. She fought against it, terrified that Richard may re-awaken. It was then that the tears fell silently down her cheeks. She tasted the salt on her lips. Her mind was filled with questions to which only Richard could supply the answers. What did it all mean? What was wrong? Something must be terribly wrong. Richard had never been in a state like that before. He used to be so happy-go-lucky and jolly at one time. Why had he said that he was no darned good? And had he really meant it when he had said he was going to end it all? Despite his muddled manner, Marguerite believed that he had intended to end it.

"There was such a tragic look of desperation in his eyes when he had looked at her. It was terrible. Instinctively she knew that their marriage was in danger of shipwreck. Poor Marguerite was in turmoil. She couldn't think what to do about it all. If only she knew. She loved Richard deeply, and was sure that he loved her and the babies. Then she began to take another line of thought. Those 'boys' with whom he spent so many of his leisure hours. She had met two of these so-called friends of his, and they were both several years older than he. Blasé she thought them, and although Richard assured her that they were both good sports, she had not liked them from the start. She thought that it was they who had led him into drinking. Richard never cared for intoxicants before he became so friendly with George Mumford and Henry Wilmot. Marguerite realised that she would have to beg Richard to give up these rogues, especially as she would be free to go out with him herself in the evenings, soon. Dear Richard, she comforted herself, he was all right really. Perhaps he was just a little too easily led, that was all. After what had happened, she would try to influence him for the better. Soon they would be happy, and all-in-all to each other, just as they were when they were first married. Then doubts crept stealthily back into her mind. Had the babies made a difference? But she refuted the suggestion as soon as it took shape. Richard was immensely proud of his son and daughter, of course he was.

"Marguerite came back to earth with a start. My gosh, what a blessing that Richard had been so quiet. If there was any real scuffle or disturbance, the family downstairs would have heard, and come up to see what the matter was. And then, she would not for worlds let them know what had occurred, it would be such a dreadful worry for them. No one must ever know. Everything would be all right in the morning. With a hundred muddled thoughts circulating in her troubled mind, Marguerite fell asleep, totally exhausted.

"It seemed only a moment that she had slept, when a whimpering in the room next door indicated that the baby had awakened to be fed. Her eyes were red and felt heavy, as though she too had been out into the early hours drinking spirits. She attended to the baby as quietly as possible, but Richard stirred. He sat up dazedly and looked at his shirt sleeves. Without a word he got up, finished undressing and got into bed again. Marguerite finished tending the baby and returned him to his cradle. She went back to bed and lay down beside Richard.

"There was an endless silence, with Richard stroking his much troubled brow. At last he whispered his wife's name and she quietly replied. Still anxious, yet calm, he started to tell her what a beast she must think him, and how he wouldn't be surprised if she hated him for it. She hushed him, urging that of course she didn't think him a beast. With a lump in her throat she leaned over and kissed him. She tucked the bed clothes snugly about him, kissed him once more on the forehead, and turned away near to tears. Continually she consoled herself, it was all right, Richard was all right.

"Later that morning, the atmosphere was still very strained when Richard eventually asked for the gun. Suddenly all her fears returned as she persuaded him that he didn't need that dreadful thing. Richard soon put her mind at rest, assuring her that whatever he might have been going to do the night before, was far removed from his mind now: 'Thanks to you, Daisy.'

"Swiftly and with new elation, she went over to Richard who swept her into his arms and kissed her tenderly. He overwhelmed her with apologies, over and over again. She quieted him and trembled with happiness. This was her own Richard once more. He told her what a darling she was, and said that he would be coming home from work early so that they could sort things out."

Parting

That day must have been cold and bleak outside in Cambridge Street. I can imagine the late January frost to have frozen over the trampled slush which glinted for awhile, as the sun made a feeble attempt to penetrate the cold clouds. I can see Marguerite in my mind, young, drawn. As her day begins, she slides back the curtains and looks down onto the scene below. All is quieter than usual, except for the occasional rumble of cart wheels, the casual tradesman, clip-clop of the horses' hooves. My grandmother loved animals, so I dwell on a horse. Did she watch the dragon smoke from its flared nostrils huff into the air and curl into nothingness? These images are very likely in Belgravia in the year 1909, everyday routines which vibrate as forgotten imprints from the past. The horse in my mind suddenly whinnies, and I am back with my grandmother's anxieties.

"The remainder of that day was a busy one for Marguerite. She became very involved with the children and the household chores, in a strict endeavour to keep her worries at bay. She had a resilient nature, and the thought of spending the evening with Richard pleased her. Even if they were going to sort things out, a solution could be found for his problems. At least she felt that he still loved her, as he had assured her earlier that morning.

"But sadly for Marguerite all was not sorted out. The problem was merely swept under the carpet. That evening Richard came home from the office looking just as worn as before. Words cannot weave an adequate picture of Marguerite's distress when he told her that he would be leaving the country. He was forced to do so because of his outstanding gambling debts, and worse. If he remained in the country the least that would happen was that he would lose his job, bringing disgrace upon his innocent wife and family. Numbly, Marguerite sensed that he was in even deeper trouble than he cared to admit. She felt a shadow of shame fall across her life.

"First of all Marguerite couldn't accept that Richard meant to leave her and her darling babies. She cried hysterically, pleading with him that she would rather anything than that he should go. But Richard was adamant. He helped her gather her senses when he told her that it would not be for long, a few weeks, maybe months and he would get a job somewhere, settle down and send for her and the little ones. Then he promised that they would be able to make a fresh start.

"Marguerite wiped her raw eyes. She realised that she had no alternative than to accept the situation for what it was. Numbly, she shuffled around the house attending to the needs of the infants. There seemed to be a corner in her heart that felt that she would never see her husband again if he left the country. Yet the majority of space was filled with her dreams of a far-off land, where she, her two babies and Richard would walk off into the sunshine together. It was those few reassuring thoughts that kept her going for the remainder of the time, until . . .

"A last wave of the hand at the corner and he was gone!

Marguerite stood quite still for a while at the gate, and then realisation came to her. We would not see him again for weeks, probably months, quite possibly years. Her Richard had gone, hoping to get a boat for America or the Far East. How dreadful to realise that now that she and the babies were alone. She felt stunned, as though a heavy blow had fallen. One more look at the corner that had swallowed her husband up, the same one that swallowed her father not so long ago, and Marguerite turned and walked lifelessly up the path. Her sister-in-law met her at the door, having arranged to stay for a few days to give Marguerite a chance to get over the worst of it. She told Marguerite to cheer up, and as she said it, she almost wished she hadn't. It seemed such a futile thing to say. She reminded the weeping girl that soon they would be together as Richard had promised. She put her arms round Marguerite, who was sobbing pathetically by now. Crying could only bring relief, she told her.

"A baby cried suddenly, a lusty newly-awakened call for immediate attention. Marguerite, now quite shattered, lifted her tear-stained face, indicating that baby Charles needed her. Hastily wiping her eyes, she climbed the stairs to her two-month old son. And that was how she began facing the new and lonely life which was thrust upon her after less than three years marriage."

The Man in a Bowler Hat

"Something of the terrible shock had worn off after the first few weeks of Richard's departure. Marguerite and he corresponded frequently, Richard telling her of his good fortune in finding work. And Marguerite began to buck up as she dreamed of a new home for them all overseas. Those days she was often a dreamer. How could she possibly be anything else? Perhaps they would settle in the Far East, America . . . She continued to dream.

"It was obvious that it would not be convenient for Richard to send for her just yet, and so a month later, Marguerite was offered her old job back at the office. Something could be worked out for the babies. The aunts could help out, or perhaps she could employ a nanny.

"Anne Ackerman was utterly stunned at the turn of events, even though she had had presentiments of disaster with regard to her daughter's marriage to this unreliable young man. Yet although she was willing to help Marguerite all she could, she too was desolate, had comparatively recently lost her own husband. It was only five years since she waved him goodbye and she was still mourning him. She was always dressed neatly in black. She adored her grandchildren, those poor, dear little ones whose father was gallivanting across the other side of the world.

"And so for the time being, it was decided that Marguerite should return to work. After all, she needed the money. Richard left her very little and not a lot came through the post. Times were hard indeed. Perhaps she would have to work for a year, or even two, until Richard got things properly sorted out. My God! A year or two without her beloved Richard. How could she – how would she endure the wretched pulsation of every lonely minute? The answer must be work. She arranged for the little ones to be cared for during the daytime. She hated leaving them, especially the little boy who was only three months old, but it was something that had to be done. They all had to eat. And realising how dependent the babies were on her, and that she would be doing it for them, eased her guilt.

"Despite having a tremendous love for the theatre, Marguerite enjoyed her work at the office. She was an intelligent secretary, and needed the mental stimulation that it offered as well as the financial rewards. On her return to work after nearly three years' absence, it was good to find that everyone was glad to see her back in the business world.

"By degrees, the hurt at leaving the babies lessened. They were so sweet, and seemed to understand the inevitability of their mother going away every morning and not coming home until bedtime. Marguerite did everything possible for them, all the precious little things that mothers love doing for their babies. But life then was very exhausting at times, especially when the baby started teething. She would sit up for hours with him during the night trying to comfort him. And when she was tired in the morning, business had to be faced just the same. Yet through all this strife, and still missing Richard painfully, she never asked or expected any form of indulgence. Her whole life at that time was work, work and still more work.

"In the evenings, after her mother hastened off to the Haymarket, Marguerite would sit down and write long, affectionate letters to Richard. His replies were enthusiastic about the new life he was living in China. The future looked bright for him, but nothing was finalised as far as his family was concerned."

It was now that a shadow fell on a house already full of anguish. Its owner was a "distasteful" man in a bowler hat. Very soon he had intruded into the hallway. He was not a stylish man. After all, he wore a bowler hat, and, according to the *Tailor and Cutter* (1909), a trusty fashion publication of the time: "The bowler hat is an abomination to the individualist in head-covering . . . tasteless depravity and follow-my-leader . . . Men of individuality eschew it and never give it peg room on the hat stand."[3] My grandmother was a woman of style. I can imagine her looking askance as the intrusive wretch claimed his peg room.

I sense muffled footsteps as Marguerite, with an air of secrecy, shows the man upstairs into the top flat. Given the circumstances of Richard's escaping the country with such haste, perhaps she feared he was a plain clothes policeman or a private investigator sniffing out payment for Richard's debts; but the man had been drinking and had the mark of a ne'er-do-well. Marguerite does not name the wretch directly, but hints that the bullying owner of the bowler hat was George Wilmot or Henry Mumford – one of his infamous friends from the swarming underworld of Edwardian London.

She continues her narrative: "It was about that time that another cruel blow fell. One evening, Marguerite received a

[3] London: Methuen, 1979 *A History of English Costume* by Iris Brooke.

visit from one of Richard's so-called friends. He said that he would like to keep in touch with Richard, but Marguerite felt that she would be best advised not to give him the address. She hoped that her husband had broken away from the old way of life. She did not want any of those men to gather him into their evil clutches and drag him down again. She was convinced that it was Henry Mumford and George Wilmot who led her Richard into bad ways in the first place. But for those two, her little family would still be all together.

"She loathed the man at first sight. He had the look of drink about his face, which in itself was unpleasant, untrustworthy. At first he tried to be pleasant, but when he could not get the information he wanted his manner changed. He became ugly and threatening. He told Marguerite that she was far too anxious to "screen" that husband of hers. Marguerite assured him politely, yet coldly, that she had no wish to "screen" him, whatever that might mean. He argued about it harassingly, constantly demanding the address and using threatening language. Eventually, realising that he was unable to glean the information he sought, he tried different tactics. He became completely and utterly hard-hearted, with not a glimmer of compassion for Marguerite who had suffered enough trouble as it was. He meant to break her. Perhaps Richard owed him money or something. He hovered at the door, and then asked Marguerite if she knew that her "fine husband" was carrying on with another girl before he went away!

"Marguerite turned towards him fiercely. How dare he come to her with such dreadful lies? "It's an abominable falsehood!" she screamed, and told him to get out of her house.

"For a moment she thought that the distasteful character was going to attack her. But he looked at her with ice-cold eyes, plucked his bowler hat from the hall stand and made his way to the front door. And then he told her that, all the same, whatever she thought of him, he had told the truth about Richard's affair, and again she shouted 'Get out!'

"As soon as the unwelcome visitor had gone, Marguerite's fury vanished as though it had accompanied him out of the door. She tried to think. It could not be true, of course. Or could it? She knew that he had been keeping very late hours, but hoped that he had been with his men friends. He had certainly been drinking and playing cards perhaps, but with a woman? Never! Of course it was absurd, she thought. Why would Richard want to spend his time with other women when he had a good and faithful wife waiting for him? Besides, there were the babies. She contented herself that he only said it for revenge, when he was unable to obtain the address from her. Yet she was very glad that she had not given in. If those were the "good friends" about whom Richard spoke so highly, she little wondered that he had got himself into so much trouble.

"By degrees Marguerite calmed down. She made up her mind to write at once to Richard, telling him of her unpleasant interview. And then she satisfied herself that she would have his assurance that it was just a despicable lie.

"She waited anxiously for Richard's answer. Not because she feared it, but because she wanted the matter settled once and for all and banished completely from her mind. A statement like that was bound to rankle until disposed of finally and forever. How long the weeks seemed before her letter would reach Richard and his reply come back to her. But at long last the letter did arrive, an event never to be forgotten.

"One day, after a long spell of work, she arrived home; and before she took off her hat and coat, she stooped down and picked up a letter from the door mat. Hurriedly she ripped it open, impatient to read the reassuring words of comfort. Quickly she scanned the preliminaries, and then whitened as she read his confession. He had admitted it! As she read on, her heart went quite cold. All the time spent waiting alone for her husband thinking that he was just playing cards with his friends, and he was keeping the company of another woman! It was cruel, cruel. Marguerite knew that she had been fooled. All that time when she was at home caring for the babies, unable to go out herself, Richard was in the arms of another woman. It seemed so unfair, for she could not freely gad about at night with the little ones to consider. She felt that Richard's love was hers by right, and that he had abused her trust.

"Over and over again Marguerite read Richard's letter through to make sure that she had not misread, that there could not possibly be a mistake. In doing so, she convinced herself that everything was only too true. But Richard had humbly apologised, promised his doubting wife that it was all over and asked that he might be forgiven.

"All night long she laid awake tossing and turning, wondering what she ought to do. What should she say in reply to the letter? After the first shock she was able to think more clearly and calmly. She started to wonder about the other girl. Richard had mentioned in his letter that she was pretty, and Marguerite supposed that that should excuse him a little. A pretty girl and a temptress! She at once saw how weak some men were if they had the mind to be. And women, some women, that is, could do a lot of harm if they chose. She wondered whether this phantom woman loved her Richard, or had she merely wanted to amuse herself with him for a few nights? After all, Richard was so young and handsome, and could be very fascinating when he chose. Was it really all over? Could his helpless little wife find it in her heart to forgive, and at least try to forget? She had continued to love her husband passionately through all that had been, and longed to see him so that she could hear from his own lips that he was truly free from infatuation. But knowing that Richard was thousands of miles away, and maybe very much alone, Marguerite knew that she could not withhold the forgiveness that he asked.

"The next day, Marguerite wrote a long letter to her wayfaring husband. Only Richard ever knew the words that were written. It was an uneasy task for her. After all, another woman had had a laugh on her and it hurt. But in her letter she had forgiven, and must now try to forget. Yet throughout all this stress, still the dreams of the new home were wavering above her head – somewhere far on the distant horizon.

"Through the weeks that followed, Marguerite settled down to hard work all day. The dreary months that came and went passed somehow. There seemed no immediate prospect of herself and her little ones being able to join Richard, as he was rather unsettled at the time. He was short of money, and it seemed hopeless for him to try to make a home where he was.

"Sometime later, Marguerite heard that he would be heading for America to try his luck in the theatre. Again she awaited news of her husband, and when a letter arrived, it came from a corner of the world still further away. But with his usual luck and charm, he had at least managed to get a job, and Marguerite seemed to think that they had got over their unhappy episode. At least, she knew that she had almost forgotten.

"Then after a while, having soared above the depression that had partnered her for so long, Richard wrote telling of yet another move, and Marguerite began to doubt whether he would ever settle down. As soon as he showed any sign of making headway, he would find the work irksome or get tired of the place itself. Then he simply drifted around from place to place again. At one time he managed to secure a decent job, although it was not a suitable place to invite his wife and children. By now, she was beginning to despair.

"Yet Marguerite herself was doing well at her job. She was making enough money to keep herself and the babies comfortably, though life was very lonely. The babies were always just off to bed when their mother arrived home from the office. And Grandmamma was usually champing at the bit to get to the Haymarket on time. There was not much company for her at all, apart from the sleeping babies. In the evenings she would sometimes sit at the table in the lamplight, pull out her writing case and write the latest journal to her far-away husband."

After my father read his mother's account of the violent circumstances at the time of his birth and of her early struggles while he had lain in his cot, he was visibly shaken. "It explains rather a lot," he said with the nod of a sage. A few days later, he wandered over to my wall and looked at a copy of his mother's picture which hung there. He suffered much in the years after his father left the family, and there is little doubt that it had set him back in life. Yet he was a philosophic soul, and never one to hold a grudge. He remained silent for a long while before saying: "Look at the wistful expression on her face. I believe it was as though she willed me to write some of my poetry." Then, almost inaudibly, he spoke his inverted sonnet, 'Shackles'. It could have been written about the tragic love affair and his mother's longing for Richard to return.

It spread wide wings in ecstasy,
The love born from a dream's domain,
Yet when the dear thing came to me
I bound it fast with link and chain,
Too soon in wistful eyes to see
Dim tears, and distant blurs of pain.

Oh, could it steal to me again?
How godly-wise to help it go
To bring new rapture from the skies
To share through dawn and even glow,
For as the homing pigeon flies
Safe to its haven now I know,
That love through love sets true love free,
And by love must return to me.[4]

When I asked my father to write about the fascinating story, he declined. He felt that it was "much too near the bone". All the same, neither he nor my Aunt Phyllis had any objections when I began to gather information. They actively helped in any way they could, rooting out old photographs and documents and telling their individual stories.

Like my grandmother, I was a romantic – in the deep sense of the word, and like her, I had an appreciation of my father's poetry. I had discovered his work shortly before the memoirs came to light, making it my business to collect the poems together and edit them for publication. Perhaps this will help to explain why I became so obsessed with those early days. At the time I was giving regular poetry readings and dramatic readings from the memoirs.

My principal interest was what effect the family drama had had on my father as a writer. But very soon I learned to

---

[4] Bristol: Redcliffe Press, 1979. Charles Ackerman Berry. *Threshold.*

distance myself and shake off the emotional ties; to be single-minded and blink back the tears that I so often wanted to shed.

The story would not allow me to rest. Waking or sleeping, I couldn't get Richard and Marguerite out of my mind. My imagination played out a costume drama, changing the old sepia photographs to full Technicolor. Then, one night, after I had been lying awake trying to piece things together, I fell asleep, and, light of step, my grandmother wove in and out of my dreams. I hardly saw her face; her white blouse was the focus of her form. But as soon as she drew near, she turned another corner and another . . . Eventually, I caught up with her as she swung through a revolving glass doorway not far from the big house in Belgravia. It would be easy to dismiss the image as only a dream, but I decided to tell my father. "Good God," he said, "that was the Eccleston Hotel!" The old Eccleston Hotel no longer stands.

I wonder when she visited the Eccleston Hotel, and what she was doing? Perhaps she was going for tea with John, the tall, distinguished man with whom she had had a liaison. Four years or more after Richard left, he still had not sent for his family. What on earth could he expect? He had all but abandoned them. Marguerite was "restless and brooded". Many years later, when she had given up all hope of their new life together in a far-off country, she sat down with her writing case and began her story. "I picked up my pen and laughed a little. It seems so silly to be writing now. . ." (I get the impression that she stopped this account started it again some while later).

She begins again: "Confessions . . . Dick, when I let you walk out of my life I little knew what it was going to mean to me. It must be remembered that I was only a young girl of twenty three, and so far had not had much fun out of life.

Marguerite, c.1911

I wished that you and I could always be together, and yet you were right across the other side of the world. I was a wife, and yet I was not a wife. And for me, Sundays were the joyous days when I had Phyllis and baby Charles with me all day long. I was able to take them out in the perambulator and play with them. But Sundays only came once a week. I should not have been denied those natural joys which were mine so seldom. The week days were beginning to get on my nerves, and my work now offered little consolation. If only I could have had something to look forward to at that time, perhaps I should not have been quite so depressed. But for me there seemed to be nothing other than work, work, and still more work and an interminably lonely void in between. I was restless and brooded.

"At about that time in question, one spring evening, I happened to walk down the office stairs and into the street with a gentleman from one of the other offices. His name was John. We fell into step together and began to talk. We chatted about all sorts of things, but when John suddenly looked up and asked me where my husband was, I felt very embarrassed. Because the firm knew all there was to know about my circumstances, I had already taken it for granted that John did also. I twisted my wedding ring uneasily, and told him that my husband had gone away abroad. John shook his head, unable to understand how anyone could be as foolish to leave such a beautiful little wife behind him. I assured him that I was going to join you as soon as possible, when the babies were a little bit older. At that John gasped, for he hardly thought me old enough to have one child, let alone two. And I told him about my darling little ones. He listened with interest. Then he said that he would be delighted if I would take a little dinner with him the following evening, and I accepted.

"The next day, all day long I seemed to be waiting for six o'clock. It was an unusual state for me to be in, as I was generally interested in my work, never bothering much about the time. At last six o'clock struck on the wheezy old clock, and I was able to start clearing away for the night. I put on a neat little frock and my best hat and coat. Although I knew I was not smart, I felt fairly presentable. I said goodnight to the others and went downstairs to the front door, trying hard to control my excitement. I walked down into the direction of our meeting place, but before I got there I noticed that John was already making his way towards me. He was tall and distinguished looking. I felt very proud when he came over to me, and flattered when he raised his hat!

"It was, of course, much too early for dinner, so he suggested that perhaps we could take a short walk in the park. We strolled towards Admiralty Arch, and presently entered Green Park, which looked beautiful. The trees were newly-green with their fresh young leaves and there was a sparkle on the lake. The spring evening was exhilarating and pleasing after a stuffy day in the musty old office. For once I really began to enjoy myself.

"Soon I learned that we were going to dine in a popular little restaurant in Soho. This pleased me immensely, for I had often read about the little Bohemian places in Soho, and always wanted to visit one. John evidently knew Soho well, because the restaurant selected was certainly very comfortable. There were soft red lights and flowers on the table. He led us to a corner seat, where I could see everything that was going on around, without me being so conspicuous. I swore that I would never forget that dinner. The food was different to anything I had ever tasted. The wine was plentiful and good.

"Towards the end of our meal I was feeling very carefree, and began to realise that I had been missing an awful lot in life. This surely was living; the wine, the lights, the movement of the people. All the while John kept looking across the table admiringly. I was flushed with excitement and the effect of the wine. My eyes sparkled for more than once when John whispered across the table, "Little bright eyes!" That, of course, made me flush even more!

"We sat for quite a long time over coffee and cigarettes, and John related some of his own history. It appeared that he was unhappily married and lived apart from his wife. I suppose I ought to have been warned, but was not at the time. I was sympathetic, not being able to understand why any woman would want to make such a charming man unhappy. He was very kind, attentive and understanding. I felt sure that he must be a very good husband. The fault could not be his.

"John continued to pay me compliments throughout the evening. I reminded him that I loved my husband and babies, and that we hoped to be together again soon. John said that he hadn't forgotten, but you were a lucky fellow to have such a beautiful and faithful wife. I didn't like the turn that the conversation was taking, and suggested that perhaps it was time we left. After all, I wanted to get back to the babies. John agreed. It was time to go.

"Once outside the restaurant I thanked John, saying that I had had a very pleasant evening. I smiled and there was an empty silence for a moment. John asked the inevitable question, whether or not I would like to go somewhere with him another evening. He told me how much he had enjoyed my company and that perhaps I could find it in my heart to take pity on his loneliness again. He took my arm and anxiously guided me across the busy road, weaving in and out of the carts and trams. He looked down at my face as we reached the other side of the road. Well why not, I thought to myself. What harm could be done? There would be no harm in my dining with him again if he liked my company so much. And I had certainly enjoyed being taken out and paid such attention. I went in leaps and bounds. It felt good that I was at least attractive to someone else. There was little comfort in sitting at home night after night, writing letters which would not be answered for several weeks. And so, like a silly fool, I told him that I would love to. John squeezed my arm and told me that I was over-kind, asking if perhaps he could accompany me home. The night was still early and so I refused the offer, telling him that I was quite able to take care of myself.

"John, hat in hand, saw me onto the omnibus. He watched it safely up the road and out of sight. Once upon the bus, I felt strangely thrilled. After all, he was very kind to me and treated me as something precious. It was a wonderful change after two years without anyone to remind me that I was still young and pretty.

"However loving your letters were, Dick, they were such a poor substitute for a woman who desperately needed real love. I used to pour out pages of love and dreams to you, but by the time they had reached you and you answered them, the moment had gone, the flame cooled down. I wanted you all the time, to feel your arms around me and your kisses on my lips. And I wanted to share the babies with you. The other woman was constantly on my mind, and I felt as though I wanted to chase her away, obliterate her memory for good. I sometimes began to wonder whether you would ever send for us.

"I had thought about all sorts of things during the bus journey home . . ."

The omnibuses were the open-topped kind, which, according to her children, Marguerite enjoyed. It was a fine evening, so I sense my grandmother's slight form climbing the winding stair and slipping into her seat. She is wearing the outfit from the photograph that hangs on my wall; her stylish hat with the delicate lilies falling about the crown, and the same neat buttoned dress with the modest lace collar. She is conscious of style, but can no longer afford to indulge herself in the latest fashion. After all, Richard was sending very little. She had two little ones to feed and clothe, and, by all accounts, she needed the means to pay for a nanny. I imagine her looking down onto the scene below. She pays no heed to the suffragettes who whirl past the Buckingham Palace Road waving their *Votes for Women* placards. Her younger sister, Dorothy, would have argued their case, but Marguerite had faith in her own intellect and did not care for sexual politics. She would not wear a tie and smoke cheroots. Let them carry on with it if they chose, but she had other, more emotional, matters on her mind. She tosses her head and the delicate lilies tremble a little.

There is something about wheels in motion that draw attention to the march of time. I wonder what other thoughts coursed through this young woman's mind as she travelled from Soho towards Belgravia. It was over two years since Richard left and time was passing without mercy. Who was he with, and what was he doing now? Did he hold her image as close to him as she held his? Surely he wondered about the children and ached for them to be reunited? Neither of them had the immediate funds for a passage to America. Fate was triumphant and Time now wore a devilish grin. Would Richard send for them while she was still young? John's compliments aside, with the stress of the last few years the bloom in her cheeks was fading. There is so much to think about and she is beginning to feel ill. She dismounts and treads the short distance past St. Saviours, the squat church on the corner.

The hand that holds the pen decades into the future trembles. Perhaps she unearthed these thoughts and paused for a moment as she sat at her table recalling that bus journey as she looked out to sea. Again she writes . . .

"On my arrival I let myself into the big silent house and crept upstairs into my rooms. I didn't want to wake the sleeping babies who were fast asleep in the room adjoining mine. How sweet they looked, and how I adored them. There was little Phyllis with her fair curls spread over the pillow, her sweet face flushed with sleep, and the baby with his rosy cheeks and red lips, his mischievous eyes now veiled by his long, dark lashes. Phyllis grew more like her daddy, and the boy, it was said, was so much like his mummy. I felt sad when I thought of the three of us, and the fourth at that moment was thousands of miles away. Yet that night was the first of many more."

Marguerite reacted wilfully to her situation. How dared her husband abscond, leaving her with two babies to care and provide for with very little income? Who could blame her for wanting to spread her wings even if she had done so for devilment? Besides, spring had blossomed, and it was just the time to stroll arm-in-arm with a "distinguished gentleman" in Green Park or St. James's. Perhaps they would have dinner later in that little Bohemian restaurant in Soho . . .

Her confession continues: "I decided to go out as often as I was asked. I could see no harm in it, knowing full well that I couldn't do anything by staying at home and brooding. I needed the outlet and began to look forward to my evenings. My friendship with John, by now, had advanced considerably. I felt that somehow we were kindred spirits, because he was just as lonely as me really. He confided in me about his past life, and how his aims and ambitions were thwarted by his wife who could not understand him. In return, I confided about my own tragedy. He was very kind and sympathetic.

"I did not write to tell you of my friendship with John. I was afraid that you would misunderstand my motive and be jealous, as you usually did. You were always very possessive and jealous without cause. Yet somehow I wondered whether you knew. Perhaps the tone of my letters was different at that time.

"One morning a letter arrived from you, in which you criticized me over some trivial money transaction. I became furious and resentful. I felt that you neither understood nor cared, otherwise you would not have hurt me like you had done. Perhaps I was ready for a quarrel. My head had been turned by flattery, and I had the idea planted firmly in my head that I could do no wrong.

"This night, however, it was different, and I encouraged it all. I stayed out later than usual, and instead of taking the omnibus, allowed John to hire a cab and accompany me home. We were being driven through one of the deserted parks and suddenly he kissed me! What a strange kiss. I had expected to be thrilled but was not, and I told him so. His kiss had subdued me. I realised that it was one thing to flirt, but a kiss was always something very special to me. Suddenly it woke me up and I was painfully aware that I was not with you. I hated myself for having allowed such a kiss to occur in the first place. John looked rather hurt as he had probably never been told before that his kisses didn't thrill.

"I apologised politely but added that he should not have kissed me. John became humble and asked forgiveness, saying that he hadn't been able to help it because I was so sweet and was meant to be loved. I replied indignantly that I was loved – by you. John added cleverly that you had a very odd way of showing your love, going off overseas the way you had done. I could see that the way things were going could only lead to tensions. And a heated argument was something that I wanted to avoid at this point in time. I urged him not to continue with the conversation, to forget it, and in turn I would forget his advances. He replied sombrely that he wouldn't be able to forget the incident . . ."

The lone clopping of a horse drawing a two-wheeled cab through St. James's Park is easy to imagine. There were still hansoms in London at that time and St. James's was in the right direction. It would be hardly likely that a motor vehicle would have veered from the known route and driven beside the duck ponds.

John wanted to get Marguerite alone and she naively went along with it. Perhaps the intentions of this "distinguished gentleman" were not entirely honourable. He flattered her when her self-esteem was low, and I get the feeling that he was hoping for a mistress. He had, after all, confided in the old cliché that his wife did not understand him. All the same, Marguerite had allowed "the kiss to occur", and after she arrived home she was tormented by guilt . . .

"That night my feelings were very mixed. I peeped into the sleeping babies and felt that I had betrayed them in some way. I crept back into my room and glanced at your photograph. And then I remembered that unfriendly letter that I had received from you that morning and felt different. After all, I was young and had been left alone. I had done nothing to deserve my plight. I was always good and loving, yet had been left to my own devices. I did not think it fair that you should criticize what I did with my own, hard-earned money. After all, you had been such a spendthrift, constantly enjoying yourself while your wife and little ones waited patiently at home. Why shouldn't I have a little fun now? Why on earth should I feel so guilty about it?

"When eventually I got to bed and turned off the light, I cried. Everything seemed so hopeless. I knew in my heart that I loved you. Another man had kissed me passionately, and I had not wanted him to."

Daisy is Missing

It was 1913. Marguerite's secret encounter with John had ended over a year ago. It was inevitable. He was a married man and she was a married lady still in love with her far-away husband. There would be no-one else for her while Richard waited on the horizon. So life reverted to the tedium of everyday routine. Then a blow fell, a blow that Richard surely knew about. While he was adventuring, he must have received a letter telling him that his wife and mother-in-law would soon be forced to move out of the big house in Belgravia. It was a family home, which I suppose attracted many claimants and ultimately it would be sold. Anne Ackerman, who was very hard up now, was forced to take rooms in Victoria, and his wife and children were almost homeless. Had he any idea what his children were about to suffer? The cold fact is that they were virtually abandoned as the result of his desertion. It seems obvious now that he had felt tied down and had never intended to send for his family, but we can never know how he really felt as things went from bad to worse. The fraught letters during that time were burned to a cinder long ago, but Marguerite, already in deep depression, now felt utterly abandoned. No doubt the humiliation that she felt within the family, because of Richard's conduct, added to the

Marguerite, whose stage name is unknown, in 'Good Evening',
Palace Theatre, c.1915

strain. I strongly sense a family rift, otherwise why did she refuse to turn to her mother at this time? Moreover, she was finding it difficult to make ends meet.

It is clear from the memoirs that Richard sent little or no money from abroad, and his wife only had a woman's wage. In the light of this, we must be alerted to the fact that, at the beginning of twentieth-century England, the dreaded workhouse remained an option for people falling on hard times. There had been a few improvements to the archaic system, but it was not until after the First World War that the Poor Law broke up and significant changes were made for the better.[5]

[5] London: Longman,1974: *An Illustrated History of Modern Britain 1783-1964* Richards and Hunt.

I suggest that Marguerite was on the edge of collapse after the incident with John, and she took refuge in the make-believe world of the theatre. Added to this, she was missing for long periods during the First World War. (I have suggested the possibility of a meeting with Richard). While I cannot fully spotlight her stage career, her children's story was related to me in detail. A painful decision was made to find suitable accommodation for them. It would only be for a few weeks, until Richard had settled once and for all and was able to save enough money for their passage overseas. She had hoped that it would be America, although she recalled her horror at reading the dreadful headlines *Titanic Sinks.* Had she considered a passage on the ill-fated ship?

According to hearsay, it was the winter of 1913 that Marguerite made her regrettable arrangements. In those days, anyone – child-loving or not – could set up a business looking after children. It was a period of exploitation to a gross degree, and the following account will testify to the ill-consequences of fragile laws that paid little attention to the plight of the young. What happened next is significant in the light of a dramatic meeting in later years. As a consequence of Richard's leaving the country, Phyllis at seven-years-old and Charles not yet six, were taken from the warmth of the big house in Belgravia – to be left parentless and alone in a series of nefarious homes in post-Edwardian London.

The drama unfolds like an old black-and-white film as the lamplight flickers meagrely in the creeping fog, an image synonymous with the shadiness that it hides. As a door opens into the past, the soft whimpering of children can be heard. I must remain at a distance outside that door now, as I testify to Charles and Phyllis's heartbreaking experiences.

Thackeray College was an orphanage in Forest Hill. From Phyllis's description, the place stands Gothic in my mind: ". . . a large, foreboding building peeping from wooded grounds." She went on to recall that "if anything resembled a strict Dickensian institution, Thackeray College did." By all accounts, the place was over-crowded with unfortunate orphans, social outcasts who should have attracted pity rather than scorn. Rules were stringent, the food grossly inadequate and the children felt half-starved most of the time. Punishment was by thrashing or food withheld for the slightest offence. There was little or no recreation.

Perhaps the children could have endured the situation better if they were allowed to be together, but girls and boys were separated. This meant that Phyllis was parted from the little brother she adored, and, in turn, Charles, who relied on his big sister, missed her painfully. Phyllis wondered why they had left the big house with "miles of stairs", the "pretty silver cutlery" and the warmth of everything. Where was their mummy, their grandmamma and the kindly old gentleman with white whiskers who sat them on his knee by the fireside?

Even though they were so young at the time, in adulthood they still remembered the awful conditions that prevailed. They were huddled four or more in a bed at night, some at the top and some at the bottom. It was cold and they were hungry and thirsty. At bedtime, the only drink available came in the form of a communal mug of water. This was passed around the children who were allowed only one sip, and 'woe betide' anyone who stole more.

As she continued to delve deeply into childhood memories, Phyllis winced recalling the meanness of it all. One evening, soon after their arrival at the orphanage, hunger got the better of her. Checking the coast was clear, she crept downstairs into the huge, old-fashioned kitchen. She stole across to the black cooking-range where she noticed a pan full of mashed potato. "It may not seem very exciting," she told me once, "but it took the form of a huge banquet." She fumbled about and found a wooden spoon which she poised to dip into the pan. Suddenly the door came open to reveal the school cook. Phyllis was instantly brought to justice. She was grabbed, thrashed and sent to bed without any supper. She was left defensive and completely alone. It was a hard lesson for a hungry child to learn.

Charles could only remember snatches of life at Forest Hill. He was only an infant at the time, but he remembered a dreadful shadow passing over his life, and it was cold. There was one day, though, that he never forgot. Their mother had realised the harsh conditions in the orphanage, and packed up their belongings. Until Richard sent for them, the children were to be taken to a suitable foster home. Once more she supposed that it was only a temporary measure.

It was 1914. In August of that year war was declared and a cloud came over London. There was a great deal of military activity near Victoria. The road was an incongruous muddle of horse-carts, motor vehicles and omnibuses. Eight-year-old Phyllis saw young soldiers hefting packs on their backs, trudging about by the station; some alone, some joining groups, some kissing their loved ones goodbye. Advertisements of Kitchener pointing an accusatory finger with the injunction '*Your Country Needs YOU*' glanced down from every available bill board. How long would these young men be gone? Perhaps weeks, months or even years. It surely put Marguerite's position into perspective. Thousands of these young men would never return. Taking her children by the hand, Marguerite wove in and out of the busy traffic and jumped on an open-topped bus for Battersea. Surely she thought about Richard as they rode; how he, too, could be going away to fight, perhaps be killed. It was small mercy that he was safe – albeit "gallivanting" far from home. Or was he? She had heard that he was making his way along the Pacific North West coast to Canada.

When they arrived at their new accommodation at Mrs. Newport's, Phyllis complained that the little house was somewhat grimy; but her mother insisted that it was a roof over their heads for now. It would not be for long, the sun still glittered out at sea on the horizon with the promise of a reunion with Richard. So Marguerite (whose stage name we never knew) left the shabby scene, slipping through the stage door of a London theatre and back into the spotlight.

Mrs. Newport called herself a foster parent. In those days anyone, child-loving or not, could qualify. In Marguerite's presence, she hadn't seemed so bad, yet she concealed the most unscrupulous behaviour. Decades later, they both shuddered when she prodded them with a bony finger from the past. In this woman's charge, Charles and Phyllis remembered the lonely days of cold, hunger and hopelessness that superseded those of Thackeray College.

During the daytime they were left to roam the streets of Battersea, ill-clothed, inadequately shod and always hungry. They were fed mainly on bread and lard, while Mrs. Newport spent most of her time at the local tavern swigging ale. Sometimes, my father recalled, they were so hungry that they ran off to the market and rummaged at the backs of stalls looking for cabbage leaves. At five years old Charles had turned into a little urchin, and he even remembered picking up discarded apple cores to eat. On other occasions, they ran off to the railway sidings to play, or sat perilously high on bridges as they watched the "puffer" trains whistle and screech through the smutty tunnels. After their day spent of its careless wanderings came to a close, they were hurried up to bed, still hungry, to join the company of bugs that lurked within the filthy sheets and crawled over the walls. Both of them remembered a "shabby little room, utterly infested".

It was becoming clear that the infant Charles, who was once earmarked for the Chapel Royal, had inherited a strong, artistic thread from his mother. But how was he to develop his talent in such dire circumstances? To this end, his resourcefulness at such a young age defies belief. He loved to sketch and was trying to write, but he never had any proper paper or pencils to hand. If Mrs. Newport had given him a slate to scratch upon, it would have been something. But this did not deter the tiny lad, who would stoop down into the gutters to pick up spent matchsticks, and, with these, he formed tiny pictures and letters in the margins of discarded newspapers. At the same time, he began to teach himself to read: dog-eared copies of *The Times.*

For Richard's young children, these experiences must have been devastating. To have taken such a tumble at their tender ages was bad enough, but they were not used to poverty. The psychological impact might have proved disastrous, but it didn't. They grew up to be deeply compassionate – two of the gentlest people. The experience had a profound influence on Charles's acclaimed book and he became an expert on homelessness in later years.[6]

Again, Marguerite realised that her children were not being cared for properly and she was forced to look for a

---

[6] London: Constable, 1978. *Gentleman of the Road* by Charles Ackerman Berry.

new foster home. Mrs. Hodges lived in Edmonton with her sister. The pair seemed friendly enough and the house was clean and tidy, even though the drab Victorian décor was "a fraction morbid". Yet it was another dreadful day for the children when their mother kissed them goodbye once more and left them in another pitiless situation, deceived by the promise of their well-being. "She went off to some provincial theatre to play Maid Marion, or something," said my father, shaking his head.

From a psychological viewpoint, Edmonton was to prove the worse place endured by the children. After their mother disappeared, they were left hand-in-hand looking warily around at their new surroundings. They noticed that one of the sisters carried a stick, but it seemed to be used as a prop rather than for any contribution that it might make to her mobility.

The two sisters, who were all sweetness and light to Marguerite, began their campaign of evil almost as soon as she left the house. They nagged and progressed to beating the children with the walking stick. It must be remembered that Charles was only five or six, and Phyllis about eight years old at the time. But the little girl used to fling herself at the sisters trying to intervene as they beat her baby brother. In old-age, she often heard the re-echo of her cries: "Please, please don't hurt my little brother!" But the sisters were merciless.

They soon began to fear the pet cat. It had nothing to do with the poor cat itself, but with what it represented. The creature became a symbol of psychological discomfort for the children. The sisters would choose the child who was to be favoured on a particular day, and exclude the other one. The favoured child was 'allowed' to stroke the cat and had to make it purr loudly, while the other child was verbally abused and beaten. It became torture for the favoured child to realise that the other was being ill-treated, and the devils knew this.

The situation in Edmonton worsened. The walking-stick beatings became much more severe, and no-one could hear the children's cries for help. They wanted their beautiful mother to come and take them away, but hardly ever saw her now.

Like their predecessor, Mrs. Newport, the sisters enjoyed supping ale. They would give Charles and Phyllis a large jug to fill up at the old pub on the corner and caution them not to spill any. It was a welcome outing. Music and the carefree singing of the locals hit the air. Long they could have stayed peeping from the periphery, but once the jug was filled they were terrified of spilling the ale and returned carefully, the jug frothing at the brim.

They were hungry here, too. I must add, however, that during the war food and other requisites were scarce, and, at that time, food was (all but) rationed. Oddly, it was not officially rationed until 1918, after the war was over. Nonetheless, the situation offered a good excuse for the women to torment the children and allow them to go hungry. They were often sent to the local grocer shop with a few pennies to buy chicken food. The sisters told them that it had been swept up from the factory floors and put into sacks. Whether it was the truth or an unsavoury taunt we can never know, but my father could remember the "vile porridge mixture" that they were given to eat. Their secret joy was when they were sent to the same shop to buy bread or cheese. Food was not measured accurately in those days. Even bread was hacked haphazardly and sold in half-loaves. This meant that there was often 'make-weight' – over and above the food item. They pilfered it on the way home: a chunk of bread, a chunk of cheese, a pleasing supplement to their meagre meals.

The children constantly wondered about their father on the far horizon in some exotic and longed-for place, but the terrifying routine at Edmonton dragged on and on with the war. Where was their mother? They were beginning to think she would never come. Then, out of the blue, she paid a rare visit. They were thrilled to see her, hoping that she had come to take them away. The sisters were on their best behaviour when Marguerite arrived, and she was welcomed with a carefully polished veneer. The dining room had been transformed; its table was laid with an immaculate lace cloth with all the trimmings. They sat down together and had sausages and mashed potato for tea.

Charles was too young, Phyllis too scared, to tell the truth. After tea, their hearts sank when they realised that their mother was going to leave them again. Marguerite handed a bag of fruit and sweets to the sisters to be shared out later, kissed her children goodbye, said that she hoped they would all be with Daddy soon, and disappeared. They were stricken to see her go, but at least they had the fruit and sweets to look forward to. They waited and waited . . . No treats materialised.

One of the cruellest memories connected with Edmonton was one Christmas – most likely 1916. My aunt related the story with remembered sadness for her little brother. The magic of Christmas clung in the air and the children were restless with excitement. They hung up their stockings on Christmas Eve and eventually fell asleep, believing that Father Christmas would deliver their toys. Surely he would not forsake them?

They were so young. It is painful to visualise their bewildered faces when they awoke to empty stockings. Phyllis often discussed it with her brother in later years, but there were a lot of 'perhapses'. Perhaps the fog was too thick and somebody was unable to make the journey to Edmonton. It has been said that Marguerite was principal girl in pantomime that year: "She was playing Red-Riding Hood, or something." Perhaps she could not get away from the theatre on time. Perhaps she was ill . . . Perhaps . . . ? Why didn't the sisters fill the stockings with anything, anything at all? As it was, even Tiny Tim had a better time of it.[7] This was the most desolate Christmas Charles and Phyllis ever remembered.

On Boxing Day things brightened when Marguerite arrived with a bundle of parcels. The children were relieved to see her and delighted with the presents. They played together for a while, until Phyllis suddenly became distressed: "Where's Daddy?" Her mother gathered her children up and hugged them: "One day we shall go far across the sea to another country to find him. I promise." Richard was apart from his family like thousands of young men now, and the children were old enough to sense that something was very wrong. Soon afterwards, their mother left them in distress, and, with her eyes glistening, returned to the world of make-believe. Her dream that they would be reunited as a family again was now in question.

Charles and Phyllis turned to the toys for comfort, for they were again left to the mercy of the sisters. Phyllis had been given a Red-Riding Hood doll which she had played with constantly, but once her mother was out of earshot, the house echoed with the cries of a tormented child. One of the sisters had snatched the new doll away and placed it out of reach on a high shelf. Phyllis wept miserably when she couldn't reach it. Later that night, when she thought it was safe, she crept downstairs and tip-toed into the parlour. She took a chair, levelled it against the shelves, balanced on

---

[7] From Charles Dickens's *A Christmas Carol.*

it and stretched up. The inviting doll was looking down at her, almost in reach and her heart started to pound. Suddenly, just as she managed to get a grip on it, the door came open and she tottered. In a terrifying moment she was jerked off the chair, beaten with the walking stick and sent back to bed. The pretty doll remained on the high shelf, gazing blindly into the night.

As a young woman, Phyllis used to write children's stories for magazines. It was the awful memory of the Red-Riding Hood doll that inspired her to write a psychological thriller called 'Doll on a High Shelf'.

With their mother on the stage and their father goodness knows where, it seemed like 'out of sight, out of mind' for the unfortunate children. Yet who knows what their parents really felt? It was up to Phyllis now, and she took on the role of surrogate mother for her little brother. Often when things were unbearable, she would sit him down, put her arm around him and say, using her pet name for him: "Never mind Luke, just imagine – we're going right across the sea soon. Won't it be exciting to go in a big boat and find father?" Like their mother, the children began to dream. However, the time would arrive when a big boat would be far too vulnerable in the middle of the Atlantic during the First World War. After all, history tells us that:

> The German submarine campaign began in 1916 and u-boats were ordered to sink ships on sight, whether they were armed or unarmed, enemy or neutral, and by 1917, four hundred and twenty three allied and neutral ships were sunk . . . [8]

[8] London: Longman. *An Illustrated History of Modern Britain 1783-1964.* Richards and Hunt.

It was now that Charles, who must have been about eight-years-old, became obsessed with boats and dreamed of going to sea. He would make paper boats and sail them in puddles and imagine all the adventures that he could have, a seeming echo of the boats his father had sailed several years ago. He wanted to write his stories down but he didn't have the means. Once, when he roused from his childhood reverie he brightened and said to me: "You know the best days were when mother came to take us out. There was an aura of light about it, and one day . . ."

Phyllis remembered that, in the spring of 1916, the blossom was out and her mother had arrived unannounced to take the children away from the house for an hour or two. They visited one of the London parks, where the occasional soldier wearing khaki uniform, strolled arm-in-arm with his girl. As they sat down and enjoyed watching the ducks with their ducklings on the lake, Phyllis told Marguerite the truth about the sisters in Edmonton and how distressed they were at the thought of going back. Her mother realised that yet again she had been deceived. "You're not going back," she said. Furthermore, she determined that her children would not be let out of her sight again. A great burden had been lifted. Marguerite immediately deposited them in the hands of Richard's mother and collected their few possessions from Mrs. Hodges. They were to stay in Victoria "enjoying freshly-baked cakes" for a few weeks until something else could be arranged. Meanwhile, Grandma Berry viewed Charles, the precocious young writer, with a deal of suspicion. His conversations – all about nature and the universe, which he claimed he had considered in his cot – were not for her.

More importantly, the children were safe; but the backdrop of the Great War remained: the sights, the sounds, the ethos of war crowded in on them. Charles remembered travelling on an open-topped bus and arguing that the soldiers should be wearing red uniforms. "They don't any more," his mother said. Very likely there was a pause before he dared ask: "Now that there's a war will Daddy come home again? "Not yet dear, he's far away, but we are going to find him one day – very soon."

Phyllis had a trip to a theatre at about that time to see a final performance. She was taken back-stage afterwards and given the doll which had been used in the production. She had no idea what the play was called, but told me that she remembered her mother gliding about the house speaking random lines: "Dead, dead and never called me mother!" And there was a doll . . . I was intrigued by this and wondered which play these melodramatic lines were from.

My head spun with tales of the past and a restless night gave way to another strange dream. I was aware of my grandmother's presence. She seemed anxious to speak to me, and I asked about the performance. She settled down and gave me all the details. When I awoke, as from the River of Lethe, I forgot the name of the character she had played. I kept repeating her fragmented words over and over again: "Yes, I played . . . I played . . . elia." It was frustrating not to remember the whole name. By now I took these dreams very seriously, as they had sent feelers into the ether and brought back mysterious information more than once. With no better clue than the final syllable, I settled for the name Lobelia, the only 'elia' I could think of, and discarded the incident.

Some years later, quite by chance, I ordered a copy of *East Lynne* for professional use. When it arrived I was alerted to its alternative title: *Never Called me Mother!* The phrase rang a bell and I remembered the dream. I opened the book and quickly scanned the cast list for an 'elia' – and found one. It is probable that Marguerite Ackerman (taking a stage name) played Cornelia Carlyle. And I have a feeling that when the curtain came down on *East Lynne* she took her last bow.

The end of Marguerite's short stage career corresponded roughly with the end of World War One. She must have been with Richard in spirit. I imagine that she wrote to him to tell him about the colourful Armistice Day celebrations in London: the confetti, the festoons of bunting and the roar of the crowd, and how the three of them were almost crushed as they were carried in the great surge of flag-waving humanity thronging to Trafalgar Square. All around her, soldiers were reuniting with their lovers; there was such joy in the air, such hope. But beneath the revelry were tragedies; lovers who would never be reunited, men maimed for life.

One such young man was Frank Rhodes who was blinded in action. Marguerite helped him train to be a shorthand-typist in order that he could make a new career for himself as a secretary. Many disabled young soldiers turned to secretarial work for their living after the war was over. This young man's mother subsequently wrote a letter of thanks to Marguerite. It had been pasted into the scrap book.

The atmosphere must have re-ignited the flame of emotion in Marguerite's heart. Surely this was the wave that would sweep her and the children across the sea and into Richard's embrace, or was it? The signs were not good, but she kept her hopes alive. She had no intention of letting Richard go. Yet she was now putting things into greater perspective. She wrote at this time:

There is no sorrow, woe or fear
But someone has a deeper one.
There is no hill I have to climb
But someone treads a steeper one.

No burden ever weighs us down,
For others heavier ones must bear.
No handicaps our progress bar,
But others find a crueller share.

For the children life became much jollier. One afternoon, as a surprise, Marguerite took them to a little cinema in Wilton Road, Victoria called the Biograph. I see three silhouettes in the audience set against the flickering screen. The film is *The Vagabond*. Charlie Chaplin is playing a violin for money when a brass band starts up in loud opposition. A saloon door swings open to reveal Richard looking dapper in an Al Capone hat. He beckons the audience in before joining the revellers at the bar. It is now almost nine years since he left the country. As the music played, Marguerite apparently became more and more excited. "Look, there's your father!" she exclaimed. It was a significant glimpse of her lost love, and the first of many trips to see a silent movie. The excitement was always the same. Some years later she pasted Chaplin's photograph into her scrapbook.

But what became of the anti-hero after he had escaped the country? What was he doing during the war? And what was he doing now that it was over?

Charles and Phyllis, 1918

Adventurer

Richard was a consummate adventurer. While Marguerite was on the stage and the children were suffering in the foster homes, her husband had broken free. One excuse after the other dropped onto the doormat in those early years as he wandered the world to make his fortune. He was "mad, bad and dangerous to know", but Richard's roguery remained no bar to Marguerite's love.[9] Despite his violent conduct and the way he had made her feel ashamed by association, she had made up her mind to trust in her beloved Richard and to remain faithful to him. He had admitted his affair with "the temptress" but was penitent and begged forgiveness. Just a little longer, a month, perhaps . . . two months, she consoled herself. Still she dreamed on, little realising the danger that their two children were facing daily in the squalid foster homes in which she had placed them.

In his wife's mind, Richard was innocent and the whole world seemed set against him. Through her memoirs we know that: when he was drunk, somebody must have tricked him; when he was unfaithful to her, the woman must have been a "temptress"; when he wielded a loaded revolver, it was because he was exhausted.

[9] Lady Caroline Lamb's description of Byron

Richard somewhere in the Far East

It transpired many years later, through a conversation with my father and Wynne Ackerman, that it was Arthur Ackerman who had arranged Richard's passage abroad because his brother-in-law was in deep trouble. I don't suggest that they were bosom pals. In fact, Arthur thought Richard "a cad". If Arthur felt it necessary to help him, it must have been through loyalty to his sister and to deflect shame from the family. Aunt Wynne confided *sotto voce* that Richard had committed a felony.

It was thought that he had embezzled from the Theatre Royal, Haymarket. (I have tried to substantiate the story but it remains a mystery. When I made enquiries I was told that police records before 1920 were often destroyed. So at this point it must remain conjecture.) Nonetheless, if he did as Wynne suggested – and the smoke/fire image comes to mind – I would imagine that the misdemeanour was not discovered until well after he had disappeared into the sunset.

Marguerite corresponded with him regularly, and each letter she received she hoped would be the letter which would beckon her and her little ones overseas to begin the new life that he had promised. The words "It won't be long until your daddy sends for us . . ." re-echo throughout the early account. It is all too easy now to glance back and examine her situation objectively; to criticize her naivety. Yet when I imagine myself in her shoes, I get a terrible sinking feeling. On the stage or not, how bleak her tempting horizon really was.

But where was Richard now? I want to horse-shoe back to a time-scale roughly paralleled to Marguerite's friendship with John in 1912, or thereabouts. Richard was still caught in the busy ebb and flow of humanity that was journeying from country to country. There are pictures of him in various guises in remote parts of the world. One faded photograph shows the deck of a ship which was carrying a number of people, described by Richard as 'coolies', across an unidentifiable body of water. I wondered whether they were bound for America, as there was a huge influx of Chinese workers to America at that time. Maybe he had taken the opportunity to jump on the boat. The scrapbook shows him tousled travelling steerage. There's no real clue to what he was up to before he arrived in Hollywood in search of the dream.

Another picture in my grandmother's scrapbook shows him wearing a white sailor suit and standing against the backdrop of an Oriental garden. I magnified it and scrutinised it. To my mind, he cut the figure of a picaresque anti-hero who had scattered more than one broken heart in his wake. Scratched beneath his image are the words: *Your Old Dicky*. There's a careless squiggle after the faded signature – but no kiss. I put the magnifying glass down and pondered for a while. The message was affectionate, but surely not the sentiment of a man who, after five years let loose on the world, was still in love with his wife.

Then I had the idea of subjecting the signature to graphology. The result was predictable. The owner of the hand was said to be intelligent, ambitious, greedy and egotistic, while having erotic dreams and possessing a lowered resistance to sex excesses and perversions.

Could the photograph have been taken in China? Marguerite's memoirs firmly placed him there at about this time. After the Boxer Rebellion was quelled in 1900, there was a Free Trade agreement with China. Between then and the Japanese Invasion it was a safe and exciting place to be, and the country attracted a great deal of Western interest. Oriental goods, in great demand, were constantly being shipped to England and America. This should be considered in the light of his status as a fugitive. He needed to be as far away from England as possible and this seemed the ideal place. Although given the persistence of the police in those days, I would imagine that he still needed to keep his head down.

As I pondered over the picture, the questions came thick and fast. What was Richard up to? Could the backdrop be on a stage? I don't believe it was. His body language seemed wrong. On the other hand, he could have been relaxing on a set; but photographers also used elaborate backdrops then. Interestingly, there is something else which I believe holds a valuable clue. He also sent a head-and-shoulders portrait to Marguerite – wearing the white tunic which belonged to the same uniform. There are no dates on the photographs, so there is no way of telling which one his wife received first. What we do know is that there must have been several weeks or even months distance between their arrival in England. Furthermore, in the head-and-shoulders portrait his hair colour was unchanged. In the Oriental photograph it looks suspiciously as though he had dyed it black. In the theatre at that time they used boot-blacking as hair dye. (He had probably taken the tip from his brother-in-law. Arthur always boot-blacked his hair while he was on the stage). Yet if he had dyed his hair for an acting part, I assume it would have been black in both pictures.

We know that he was in China in those early days, but the truth is that there is nothing substantial to link his whereabouts with the Chinese backdrop. A titillating explanation, turning all theories on their head, would be that it was taken down town Los Angeles in the Chinese red-light district.

The romantic spirit in me would prefer to believe that Richard was on a remote stage somewhere in the mysterious East, but it is difficult to know what he was up to at that time. He had written to say that he wanted to try his luck in the theatre, but his moment had not come. Given the uniform, it is possible that he had found himself a job on a ferry in China or somewhere else out in that part of the world. Whatever the truth of the matter, he eventually grew restless again and wrote to Marguerite telling her that he was bound for America. Most of the evidence gleaned from then onwards is replete with significant dates.

Life weaves strange and unpredictable paths. It was 1913 when Richard crossed the Pacific bound for America, and the first port of call en route from China was San Francisco. I believe that it was here that he was keen to find work in the theatre. But there was an obstacle: he wanted American citizenship and rules and regulations were stringent. He had not entered the country through the official channels so (even if he wanted to) he could not settle with his family at this juncture. The obvious course of action would be to travel by train along the Pacific North West through Oregon and Utah and on to Canada. As a resident in the Commonwealth country for a specified period, he could then slip across the border back into America and down to Los Angeles where he was fully determined to make an impression on Chaplin. But there was another snag: war.

How Marguerite's heart must have sunk when yet another excuse not to send for his family dropped through the letterbox. I can visualise her, a sad figure separated from their children who were now in the orphanage. I find another rent into the past, and, in my vision, she has returned late from a provincial theatre. She enters a dingy little room like a set. The spotlight is still on her. There is a letter waiting for her. She picks it up and begins reading it as she removes her hat. She scans the pages eagerly, her eyes darting in the hope of recognising any sign from Richard, anything at all to give her hope. There is none. Canada has joined in the war and Richard has enlisted.

She re-reads the letter, the tears coursing down her face. She goes to her trunk and slips the latest letter into the slender bundle tied up in a blue ribbon.

Wounded

Marguerite's memoirs end her story abruptly in 1913, although her reaction to the news that Richard was destined for Europe would have made fascinating reading. So close, yet so far! How she must have willed him across the channel and back into her arms. Her heart surely missed a beat when she received the news that Richard had been wounded and was at last on his way home. But there was the question of his misdemeanour. Did she fear, unnecessarily under the circumstances of war, that a meeting with her husband in England could result in his imprisonment?

It is difficult to trace the exact circumstances of our grandfather's time in the army, but I know from pictorial evidence and from a conversation with my brother that there was truth in the rumours. He was of old a chameleon, and no click of the mouse has come up with anything. Mind you, we must bear in mind that he may have adopted more than one alias, and that he was a fugitive offers a variety of twists and turns in his story. The fact is, he wanted to be invisible, and, in truth, he remains as elusive as ever and questions remain unanswered.

In the spring of 1914, an American newspaper issued a complaint against Europe with the headlines: "Militarism

Run Stark Mad." Warning bells were surely rung for Richard and for the wife who longed to be reunited with him. The following August Britain declared war on Germany. Even if he wanted to send for them (and sadly I doubt it) there was now a serious consideration: a transatlantic crossing could not be undertaken by his family without extreme risk. Fate was playing an active part now. It is certain that Marguerite acknowledged the war as a turning point. She persisted with her dream of a reunion, but now there was a more serious turn of events.

By the time Richard reached Canada war had been declared, and some simple deduction about his antics can be carried out at this stage. There was no conscription until 1917, which means that he volunteered for the army. It is likely that he was one of 30,000 in the 1st Canadian Division of the Canadian Expeditionary Force.[10] But like hundreds of other young men who volunteered, he had no idea what he was letting himself in for. It has been said that "Eventually people learned of the horrible things happening in Europe and stopped volunteering."[11] It is most likely that he was involved in the action at Ypres in 1915. I do not rule out the battle at Somme (1916), but would this have given him time to be wounded and fit enough to be signed up for *The Vagabond* with Chaplin in 1917? I doubt it. We can safely rule out Passchendaele, which would be far too late.

He must have realised that he would be packed off to Europe if he joined the army. So what exactly was his motivation for enlisting? He could not yet realise his ambition to appear in Chaplin films so there are several possibilities. He certainly needed money and the army was

[10] Ibid.
[11] Ibid.

always an option for those displaced souls in search of bed and board. On the other hand, it has been suggested that he volunteered on the understanding that he could easily lose himself in the great swathes of khaki bound for Europe. Further, it would be easy to scoff at the idea that he simply wanted to do his duty and fight for his country. But my guess is, that equipped with wanderlust, he followed his adventurous spirit. That being the case, and the horrors of this pointless war being so, he would live to regret it. But fortunately for him, he was invalided out of the army. I have no idea of the extent of the injury, but my father suggested that Richard was the victim of a gas attack. There is a strange twist. The adventurer had escaped the country and hidden in the far-flung corners of the world only to be wounded and forced back to English shores. It must have seemed as though Fate was closing in on him.

Now comes the tantalising idea of a meeting between Marguerite and her husband. It has to be conjecture, but is it feasible that she would deny herself the opportunity to see him again? It was between 1915 and 1916. The years had passed slowly and painfully, yet she still loved her husband and claimed him as her own. She remained on the stage for a while after her children were removed from foster homes. Did she at some point during this period leave for a military hospital? I picture her receiving a letter with the heart-leaping news of Richard's arrival in England.

One Saturday night, she waits impatiently for the final curtain, smartens herself up and slips past a knot of people at the stage door. Soon she boards a train. It whistles and screeches to the coast . . . She jumps down and gets into a cab . . . She arrives at an improvised hospital and searches desperately among the injured . . . He is there slouched in a corner somewhere, pale and vulnerable. I can only imagine the heavy beating of her heart, the silence of her approach. She had expected the same Richard, but he was different. There is a long, vibrant pause as their eyes meet but he cannot hold her gaze. It is all so surreal, not what she had dreamed about. At last she speaks, but her words are not as she planned.

"You've lost that boyish look. You've aged," she tells him.

"Well, I've been in the wars, and . . . It's been a long time, Dais."

"A long time? Is that all you can say?"

"And my children?"

"Didn't you get my letter? They're with your mother – until I finish my tour."

He eases himself forward: "I think about them." He grips her arm. "I never stopped loving you, Dais."

"Richard!" She flings her arms around him, tears coursing down her cheeks. She dries her eyes and looks at him. "Everything will be alright now . . . All those wretched people . . . They'll have forgotten it all. You can come home again now." Her eyes widen with the inflection: "You are coming home?"

"God, no!"

"But now that you're here . . .Think of the children . . . " She seems to grasp at something precious as it begins to slip away.

"I can't. It's too complicated. I'm being sent back to Canada when I'm fit enough. I'm out. I'm out of the army and there's a chance for me with Chaplin. You must see that I must take this opportunity."

"You mean you're hoping for a part? You and hundreds of other actors, hoping for a part with Chaplin? Oh, be realistic."

"I am. I shall convince them I'm just what they're looking for. And you, too, Dais."

Marguerite Ackerman, c.1915

"Me?"

"Yep. Those big, melodramatic eyes. You'd knock the spots off Edna Purviance."

"But I can't . . . I just can't. It would be too dangerous for the children. Think of Lusitania.[12] And anyway, even if it was safe, we couldn't afford a passage to America."

"Look darling, the war will be over soon. I'll send for you as soon as I'm settled in Los Angeles."

"You'll send for me! How many times have I heard the same story? Have you any idea what you've put me

---

[12] In May, 1915, the liner was sunk by a German U-boat

through? The weeks, the months, the years. Well, have you, Dick? You promised me, but what is indefensible, you promised our little children. God only knows I want to trust you, but I can't, I can't!"

A nursing sister comes forward and indicates that now would be the right time to part. It is an emotional parting for Marguerite with the promise of a letter from her husband very soon.

Letters arrived without invitation. Marguerite learned that Richard sojourned in Canada long enough to cross the border back into America and claim citizenship. He travelled back down the Pacific North West to San Francisco and from there to Los Angeles. He was obviously fit enough by now to join in the well-choreographed rough and tumble with Chaplin.

Two years passed. Written on the back of a strip of photographs in Richard's slanted hand are the words: *Is this the one you wanted, darling?* I find it mysterious given that it is dated 1919, ten years or more after his departure. I wonder whether they really met as I imagined, and could they have re-kindled their love in England? It is certain that something conclusive happened shortly after the receipt of those photographs. Did Richard let her down again? The fact is, Marguerite suddenly up-rooted the children and went west – to Cornwall.

In Pictures

It is likely that Richard Percy Berry changed his name to Richard Lee when he arrived in Los Angeles. I once searched the Los Angeles telephone directory looking for possible descendants and I found columns of Lees approaching battalions. He had chosen a popular name, one to get lost by. Today, according to the internet, there are nine million Richard Lees living in America. It stands to reason that, despite being in the army, he had something to hide, and this was an ideal place to lose his identity. Soon after his arrival in Hollywood, the disguise was successfully completed – beneath thick layers of film makeup and an assortment of whiskers. A clown could hardly have done a better job.

In recent years, I was in a bookshop – searching for something completely different – when I stumbled across Chaplin's final biography, *My Life in Pictures*. I idly flicked the pages until they stopped at random. I was stunned. I had caught up with Richard Lee at last. Several years ago I had abandoned my research as I did not have enough real evidence. Now, I had accidentally found a picture of my grandfather in a scene from *A Dog's Life*. I bought the book, and, after a while, more pictures of Richard Lee surfaced, confirming chunks of his life that I could only dream about before.

I fashioned a backdrop of Hollywood. The American dream was a powerful magnet for opportunists from all over the world at that time, including Richard. Restless and kicking his feet, he arrived in Los Angeles soon after the birth of moving pictures. The hedonistic ethos of Hollywood in those early years is legendary. It was the place to be for an actor and adventurer. Today, all the actors I know are in awe of Hollywood and the old silent movies. Some years ago when I was out and about with the actor David Hemmings, we discussed film techniques and the subject turned to Chaplin. He was immediately animated and envied Richard who had arrived at such a significant moment in film history – just when the Hollywood star was on the ascendant.

Marguerite's husband had swapped the drizzle and fog of London for sunny California, and, at that time and in that place, the newly-named Richard Lee was clearly in his element. Despite Marguerite's denial, it is obvious that her husband needed no help to prise open a bottle of drink. It is well known that in pre-prohibition America the liquor flowed freely and was in plentiful supply. Even cocaine was obtainable across the counter in any drug store. (I make no assumptions here). What is more, the place was well-endowed with film starlets – or with well-endowed film starlets. One, with the delightful name of Dixie Doll, was in *A Dog's Life* with Richard. Another, Babe London, was employed by the same film company in those days. He had plenty of time on his hands, and so often I have indulged in guesswork. From what I have gleaned about his character so far, and given the picaresque image, it is all too easy to draw conclusions.

My attitude to Richard has mellowed over the years. He has lost his roguery and taken shape as a colourful Lothario. To be fair to him, he did possess an unusual charm and, according to Wynne Ackerman, "he was a fascinating

Richard (second left) with Chaplin in 'A Dog's Life', 1918

character". He surely must have had some talent as an actor. Chaplin directed many of the films in question. As an exacting director and a perfectionist, he often spent several hours on a specific movement or gesture – down to the tilt of a wrist. It is thought that Richard was involved in these early productions for about three years (1916-1919). But as a supporting actor, he did not overstretch himself. What makes it difficult to unmask him is that credit was only given to the principal actors. Richard, who was not a principal, is not listed. I am surprised that he has surfaced as often as he has, given the amount of make-up, false beards, wigs and assortment of hats that these early film actors wore. In every photograph in the scrapbook he looks different from the next, so it wasn't easy to spot him in the films.

In 1915, according to my father, who insisted that he had seen the film at a later date, Richard played a part in *The Tramp* in an earlier Essanay Company production. In view of his father being wounded in the Great War, I doubt it.

Ackerman and Wynne who were instrumental in Richard's disappearance overseas.

Very likely, *The Tramp* was confused with *The Vagabond*. It would be an easy mistake to make. He was definitely part of the Mutual Company which formed in 1916, as, with a shade of irony, he can be seen in motley company swigging shorts in a saloon in *The Vagabond* (July, 1916) and possibly, but difficult to confirm, aboard the ship in *The Immigrant* (June,1917). He surfaced again by the side of the 'Kaiser' at the wheel of a military car in the war propaganda film, *Shoulder Arms* in 1918, which must have felt quite strange after being involved, however briefly, in the conflict. He was definitely in *Charlie's Picnic* and *A Dog's Life*, both made in 1919.

As I watched the infamous Mr. Lee scampering about on celluloid and downing whiskies, I could not help sparing a thought for his two children and the wife who longed for the family to be together. The children's deprivation had not been portrayed on the screen to hoots of laughter. Theirs was once a harsh reality. As for Marguerite, in 1915 she had her photograph taken while she was appearing in *Good Evening* at the Palace Theatre, Hammersmith. Soon afterwards, she sat for a new and alluring portrait. In both studies she is heavily made up like an actress of the time, and her image is far removed from the staid young woman of 1912 with the delicate lilies in her hat. No doubt she sent copies to Richard after he arrived in Los Angeles, hoping to attract him. She must have realised that he was surrounded by alluring women – most of them melodramatic film starlets. No doubt she considered the possibility of herself as a silent movie star, tied to the rails as the train lumbered towards her, or clutching her breast in mock despair. Yet hers was a real despair. When she sank down onto a dressing room floor after receiving her husband's latest letter and rebuff, there were no sombre violins playing.

A famous picture shows Richard sitting alongside Chaplin, Edna Purviance and other notable members of the Mutual Company at that time. It is not difficult to identify Richard. With his hands slung between his thighs, his permanent body-language, he looks just like his daughter, who, according to Marguerite was "so much like her daddy". An interesting production picture from *A Dog's Life* (First National) shows Richard and other familiar Chaplin characters actors sitting on a bench. It was a still from a scene labelled: 'The Dole Queue'. He still wears the ring which he always wore on his right finger, *right* being the operative word. It was the ring that he was to give to his long-lost son (symbolically, it would appear that he never totally surrendered himself to Marguerite). I have seen him in *A Dog's Life*, 1919. There is another scene where, with a deadpan look, he is dancing with a huge woman and doesn't know quite where to place his hands. He does this with very measured, stylized movement, betraying Chaplin's hand in the direction.

Searching the scrapbook, I once peeled back a picture of Richard sitting up a tree wearing a soldier's uniform. I thought perhaps that it was taken during a break in filming, but I was wrong. It was actually taken during his time in the army. The trouble is, I sometimes wonder whether he was ever aware of his true identity. I have come up against a number of uncertainties during an endless search through yards of old film footage. Peel the thick makeup off and you are left with another mask. Despite some solid evidence, he remains characteristically elusive.

Continuing my magnified search in Chaplin's book, some interesting and substantial facts surfaced. A daily production report for June 14th, 1919 stated that the weather was "fair" and confirmed that Richard Lee was hired for a full day's work for which he was to be paid five dollars. The other actors (except for the stars) were paid two dollars and five cents for half a day's work. Something that, for some reason, made me chuckle was this: a schoolboy, called K. Zimmerman, was not put on the pay roll, but "No school today" was recorded on the production sheet. With a whole five dollars, it seems that Richard Lee was riding high. The report states that the actors were only needed for four days. The film was scheduled for three weeks, but seventeen days out of the three weeks were marked 'idle'. I smiled when I read the word. After all, it is often said that 'The Devil makes work for idle hands to do.'

After the First World War, Douglas Fairbanks (Senior), Mary Pickford and some of their contemporaries were reported to be worried about forthcoming mergers in the film industry which might adversely affect their contracts. As a result, they joined forces with Chaplin and associates to found the United Artistes Company. It was another milestone in film history. The Mutual Company folded completely after the loss of Chaplin, their box-office draw.

At the time the Hollywood pictures were taken, Richard had a wife, an eleven-year-old daughter and a ten-year-old son in England. The war was over now, and the children had been reunited with their mother. Surely if he was going to send for them it would be now. But he did not. My father told me that his mother had not given up hope of a re-union, and still read and re-read the letters which were tied up in a blue ribbon and hidden in a trunk together with all her theatrical paraphernalia.

A question mark arises here. I cannot trace any of Richard's involvement as an actor in films after the merger, a very important milestone in film history. He could well have been involved, but he needs another backdrop. I should imagine that, filming or not, he frequented the western-style saloons. Something like the setting in *The Vagabond*. It is interesting, in the light of his taste for alcohol, that the 'Anti-Saloon League' was active at the time. I suppose the more Puritanical states felt the effects more than California, but with 1920 came Prohibition and alcohol was banned throughout America until the Act was repealed in 1933.[13] I can sense the initial hue and cry, but it doesn't take much imagination to picture Richard having a sly one in one of the illicit drinking dens. He was not in the company of George Willmot and Henry Mumford, but rest assured there were others of a similar ilk more than willing to assist him. With the spurious image of Richard being muscled off, loudly protesting, to a 'speakeasy' in the company of an attractive film starlet, he remains in uncertain circumstances at the beginning of the 'Roaring Twenties'.

[13] London Cassell, 1974. *Brewer's Politics*. Nicholas Comfort.

Cornwall

Once the jubilations were over to mark the end of the war, the inevitable social upheaval followed. The populace was swelled with casualties (mental and physical): the shell-shocked, those who were sightless and limbless and the generally displaced. This led to unemployment and soaring costs.

Marguerite had been sensitive to others' suffering and this helped her to put her own life in perspective. Although things were not ideal, and she was still denied the reunion with Richard who was in Hollywood, there was some improvement as far as the welfare of her children was concerned.

Conditions were, however, very cramped in Richard's family home in Victoria where they had taken temporary lodgings. To ease the situation, twelve-year-old Phyllis was sent to work for a disorderly woman with several children who, like Mrs. Jelliby, needed an extra pair of hands.[14] Marguerite eventually withdrew the child, fearing that she was being used as a drudge.

---

[14] Mrs. Jelliby is an evangelistic character with several children in Dickens's *Bleak House.*

Meanwhile Charles, who was about ten now and owned his first pen, was often left in the company of Grandma Berry. She was kind enough and made delicious cakes, but the child felt uncomfortable in her company. He attributed it to the fact that she criticised his love of books. Books, in her opinion, never did anybody any good, and there is no doubt that she found the small boy precocious. Many years later Charles recalled hiding under her table when he was suddenly dragged out by the ear, exhibited to some aged aunts as a "scruffy urchin" and measured up for a Norfolk jacket.

After a while, a small flat became available in Victoria next door to Anne Ackerman. The children were able to communicate with Grandmamma through an adjacent balcony. For the first time in their lives Charles and Phyllis could enjoy themselves. Sometimes they would be taken to the Haymarket Theatre for tea and cakes, and, on one occasion, they were given tickets to go to the London Palladium to see Arthur in a show.

And Richard? He must have written to Marguerite about his continuing work in the Chaplin films. She often took the children on trips to the *Biograph* to see them, suddenly drawing attention to their father. But as time went on – and it is now over ten years since he left – his name was mentioned less and less. His wife was losing hold of her dream of a far-off shore and with it her grasp on her marriage. She was hoping for a future that could never be and her life was in limbo, albeit that she still cherished his letters and held them close.

In 1920 I sense that something significant happened. Did Richard write to his wife to end their relationship once and for all? Only a while ago he had called her darling. What had changed? Whatever the reason, Marguerite suddenly accepted a secretarial position in Cornwall. She made up her mind to leave London and the stage for good. Everything happened quickly. She told the children: "We're going to live by the sea." Very soon trunks were packed and they boarded a train bound for Newquay. My father recalled the journey from the train station to the little terraced house which was to be their new home.

"It was one of the most memorable moments in my life. We took a jingle from the station and could see the beach in the distance with miles and miles of golden sand. After we had unpacked a few things we went down to the harbour and out onto the beach. The sea heaved against the rocks and great rollers broke against the shore. We ran and ran . . . I looked out to sea and from then on the poetry was at my finger-tips. I knew I could write here . . ."

A faded photograph in her scrapbook shows Marguerite soon after her arrival in Cornwall. She is dressed simply in a cloche hat and woollen coat. There is a great deal of pain behind her smile and the vibrant beauty of her youth has left her. A photograph of Richard taken at about that time shows him wearing tweeds and carrying a fishing rod and basket. His face is thinner too, but he is smiling widely – like the one that got away. Marguerite finds comfort in the lives of their children, and in her walks along the headland with Paddy the dog, drawn to the drama of the sea.

In 1922, Charles won the League of Nations' essay competition. His mother, who regularly posted photographs of the children and work that they had produced, immediately wrote to Richard enclosing a copy of the essay. No doubt she received a subdued reply. Were his letters colder now? She could not expect him to remain celibate during all those years apart. Until now she had pretended differently, but this time there was a distinct whiff of another woman's perfume. Was she a temptress, or simply a much younger woman who cared for her husband?

Time ticked on, and, with each tick, it erased another dream. By 1926, Richard's letters were few and far between. Charles, himself something of an adventurer, had gone to sea and Phyllis was working as a nanny at Sandhurst. Marguerite was often alone with her own thoughts now, and she turned more and more to nature for her consolation. There was no more drama in her life as she began pasting her memories into her scrapbook. Then one day Charles wrote to her from his ship, *Scalaria*, telling of his excitement about his next big voyage – to America. What is more, he would be weighing anchor in San Francisco.

Larger-than-Life

It is 1926 before I am able to pick up the threads of Richard's life, and I shall do so as I remember the dramatic account of Charles's meeting with his long-lost father, an encounter worthy of any film script.

It was the Jazz Age. By now, Richard Lee had found himself a new and effective disguise. My father provided a valuable pen sketch. The adventurer now spoke with an American accent and had become a larger-than-life Hollywood character. He wore a floppy hat and tweeds, drove a 'Tin Lizzy' and gestured through clouds of cigar smoke.[15] Although he was the antithesis of an English gentleman, he exuded influence and charm.

There is an inkling that he explored more of America shortly after the film company mergers. It was said that he visited Oregon and the Pacific North West at about this time. From there he made his way to Canada, where I imagine him hypnotised on the edge of a bursting waterfall. An adventurer like Richard would have resisted any promptings to send for his family while he was foot-loose-and-fancy-free. At some juncture he must have jumped aboard an old pioneering train back to California

[15] An early 'T' Ford.

where he settled in San Francisco. He had been a film agent in the area for some while – perhaps since the formation of United Artistes. It was here that he met the other woman who was to put an end, once and for all, to a reunion between himself and Marguerite. It seems incredible that he was still corresponding with the wife who continued to pine for him in England. I suppose that the thought of his children, who had now grown up, was bound to haunt him from time to time. Phyllis was almost twenty. Charles was eighteen now. Surely it was a shock when he opened Marguerite's letter to learn about the imminent arrival of his son to San Francisco.

"I'll never forget the wonderful day as we neared America," my father said, "I couldn't put my finger on it, but there was something almost prophetic about it." He went on to describe the approach. The *Scalaria* cut its way through the Pacific. I can see the white foam frothing its flanks. Everything burst with colour as the ship was joined by flying fish and silvery porpoises that had risen and ducked in unison with the waves. The porpoises were uncannily friendly and acted as escorts for many miles towards the end of the journey. The sun was high and the day hot when San Francisco Bay came into view.

Meanwhile, Richard recollected that he wanted to keep abreast of his son's progress, and thumbed anxiously through the shipping news to trace the whereabouts of *Scalaria*. Later on that hot day, he tied up a few loose ends in his busy theatrical office, started up the car and motored down to the Bay.

As Charles hurried about his shipboard duties, he anticipated the adventure awaiting on the shores of America. Yet there were no thoughts of his father. As far as he was aware, Richard Berry could be anywhere in the world. His mother rarely mentioned him now. For Charles, at least, his father had curled away into nothingness long ago.

Soon after the *Scalaria* docked, the young sailor received a message that the Captain wanted to see him immediately. He was somewhat puzzled and, at the same time, apprehensive. He wondered what on earth the Captain wanted him for. He steeled himself and knocked. When he entered, he was surprised to see a third person was present, an American by all accounts "wearing ridiculous plus fours". It was an image that he later adapted for a cartoon intended for *Punch*, the humorous magazine.

It is not hard to imagine what Richard's feelings were when his grown-up son stood before him, the son who he had last seen innocently asleep in his cradle. The American stepped forward and shook the young sailor's hand, introducing himself as "Mr. Lee, a good friend of your father's," adding, "I'm gonna show you the sights of Frisco." It was then that Charles was given permission to take some shore leave with the man who, on first impressions, seemed "charming but rather gregarious, and rather conscious of his fashionable image."

Once down the gangplank, Charles made for the 'T' Ford which was parked by the side of the quay. He swung a bundle in the back and got in. Mr. Lee was uncharacteristically quiet and there was: "a certain uneasiness for a while as we drove away." The two were complete opposites, and it was evident from the outset that they had very little common ground. The situation lightened for Charles who was drawn to the scenery as Mr. Lee turned inwards towards the city.

There were people that Mr. Lee wanted Charles to meet, but before they did so he stopped off at the theatrical agency. It was typical of its kind, Charles remembered. There was a heavy desk snowed under with papers, and leaflets, posters and an assortment of promotional photographs were pinned to the wall – mainly glamour shots. Mr. Lee tidied a few things away and scribbled a few notes. A conversation ensued. My father unlocked information that had been immured in his memory for several decades. Their interchange went something like this:

"Sit down. You like the theatre?" he asked, puffing at his cigar and weighing the young man up.

"Not much, actually."

"Say, you surprise me."

"Oh, really."

"So . . . What's with the dislike?"

Charles did not want to offend his father's friend. "Not so much a dislike . . . I've been surrounded by it for so long, I suppose. It's lost its magic for me." (Charles always said this. It is not surprising that the theatre had lost its magic, given what he had suffered as a child.)

"So the theatre's lost its magic . . . Yeah, this can wait." I see him sling down the papers that he'd been fingering, wanting to give full ear to what his son was saying, "Let's get the hell outa here and go for coffee. You can tell me all about that family of yours that I've heard so much about."

It was busy in Frisco. As they stepped into the steep streets criss-crossed with trams, Charles was overwhelmed by the crazy fashion being exhibited on the street corners. Imagine the hustle and bustle of the city: men in brightly-checked plus fours, women – many of them flappers – wearing their skirts above their knees and strange arrangements in their bobbed hair. "Perhaps it was the contrast of being out at sea, but the sights, the sounds . . . everything in San Francisco moved so quickly. I hardly had a moment to collect my thoughts," said my father. "I think then that we went for an ice-cream soda or something, and we picked up our conversation."

My father was a raconteur. He repeatedly discussed the memorable meeting between himself and his father, supplying ample information about the essence of their conversations. There was plenty for them to discuss because my grandmother was a prolific letter-writer. No doubt her letters to Richard had been long and full of anecdotes. Mr. Lee had clearly been informed about most of the intimate family details, their highs and their lows. He had followed some of the theatrical exploits keenly. He must have heard about the family scandal, and allowed himself a wry smile. After a top education and scholarship to Girton College, Cambridge, Dorothy ran off with a music-hall conjuror and earned the spurious distinction as the first woman to be sawn in half. He knew all about Arthur Ackerman (who was an able actor as well as singer) being too proud and "legitimate" to have anything to do with films, and that the same brother-in-law was to embark on a world tour. He knew that Anne Ackerman had become dresser to Gertrude Lawrence, and about Marguerite's short career as an actress. There was talk that he knew about the family pets – perhaps Tirrups, the kitten they had rescued from a crash site towards the end of World War One.

Who was this friend of his father's, and why did he know so much about the family? Mr. Lee could have been a fly on the wall, without the wherewithal to cover his tracks. By this time, Charles was beginning to suspect that this outlandish character suited in gigantic checks was his father. How else would he know so much about the family – particularly himself and his sister? Closely resembling Dickens, my father was an accomplished actor, although he eschewed the stage. From his regular impressions of Richard, I have dialogue aplenty. The conversation went something like this:

To the puff of a cigar – "You sure are something, you kids. Say, didn't Phyllis rescue a child or something?"

"Or something. Actually, yes. It was in a fire at . . ."

"Sandhurst."

"Yes, she was a nanny there."

"She sure was brave."

"Yes, she's a jolly good sort."

"She sure draws pretty pictures."

"Sorry?"

"Phyllis. I gotta few."

"You have?"

"Uhu" – he has a puff of his cigar – "So what's with the writing?"

"You know I write? How did you know . . .?"

"I know. Your mother sent me those poems you got published in that magazine. And she wrote me about the literary prize. The League of Nations, huh? She sure was proud."

"Was she, though?"

"Yep. You're talented, my boy." (Moments of irony were bound to surface.)

Richard had received a magazine copy of the following poem by post some while before. Incredibly, it was written when Charles was only seventeen, and it must be appreciated in the context of the poet's early life, when he was an urchin on the streets of London cold and hungry and writing with matchsticks.

Answer

You called me lonely when you saw me by the stream,
You town-grimed wanderer from your narrow streets.
Had you not eyes to see where twilight meets
The tree-tops painted as a dream?
Had you not ears to hear the call of birds,
Or heart to feel the earth's heartbeats?

Who measures solitude by absent crowd,
Or wealth of friendship by a voicing horde?
I dwelt in loneliness where traffic roared,
Where millions strove to magnify life's nothingness
And passed life by;
I found fulfilment where the skylark soared,
Where space was empty – to the empty eye.

This is the sweet of earth,
But unconfined
Within the limits of material bars
I trace a way beyond the infinitely void,
Seeking the latent levers of the mind
To probe the mighty cauldron of the stars.
In the still night a thousand tongues I find,
In each small voice God's mystery entwined.

And here,
Borne on the worldly crust, the flowing green,
The moving pageantry, the humble might,
The changeless, ever-changing scene:
Blue sky, the white
Of cloud, the autumn gold, the pause where seasons meet,
The cosmic miracle of day and night . . .

I find a God, a breathing, living God,
While men forgetting, call their lives complete;
I sense a growing light,
I feel the depth, the breadth, the height,
The magic loveliness,
The surging soul of earth, life's bittersweet.

You called me lonely when you saw me by the stream,
You town-grimed wanderer from you narrow streets.

Richard must have been astounded when he read the poem. He was the emotional sort, but not an intellectual like his son who was a lyric poet and pantheist. Whether he fully appreciated the poem that had fallen onto his mat is open to question. "It's sad, really," said my father some years later. "He was much too gregarious for me. It stands to reason that we could never enjoy each other's company. People may not understand that it's down to vibrations, and the vibrations were completely wrong." Spiritually the two were poles apart. It was a question of the child being "father of the man", and I can feel the sadness in that.

Nonetheless, it is important to appreciate the situation from Richard's perspective. Who can tell what he truly felt? We know he had been receiving photographs of his children. We all know how time plays tricks when we bump into someone who we have not seen for many years and they are suddenly sallow and grey. I have often wondered how Richard felt when he stood face-to-face with the young man who, it appeared, had grown from baby to young man with such alarming speed. And what of his feelings when he sensed that they had very little in common? Moreover, seeing Charles in the flesh, so closely resembling his far-away wife, could have been unsettling to a degree.

According to my father, the experience in San Francisco was pure cinema, and the story he told left glimpses of Technicolor in my mind as I imagined Mr. Lee showing "the sights of Frisco". There were recollections of "flappers" in the streets by the theatrical agency, goggle-eyed men in floppy caps hooting horns – a general urgency about everything. I do not know exactly where it was that Mr. Lee revealed his true identity. There were certainly awkward moments, but being in the thick of San Francisco at the height of the Jazz Age eased the tension in those first few hours. Charles began to pace up, let his hair down, join in with the heady ethos.

That evening things happened at apace. The young sailor was spun about the city and into a dance hall where he was whirled into the Charleston. "Gee, look at that guy! Watch him go!" they shouted, "Charlie of the Charleston!" He had never seen such short dresses and eccentric fashions: zigzag-patterned couture shimmering with beads and sequins that swung and flickered as the girls danced; glittering bands and feathers – some Red Indian designs, others redolent of figures in Egyptian tombs clipped into in their bobbed hair; arms waving, fingers flicking, legs knocking together. They needed no alcohol, but they were drunk, aided and abetted by the piercing notes of the brass band. Suddenly, to the note of a trumpet, I imagine a string of beads breaking loose and rolling over the floor, scattering in all directions. Charles joins in the mad scramble to gather them up. He had noticed the zany wearer and she had noticed him. They crawl towards each other on their knees chasing beads. Their eyes meet. It is Ola.

I learned that tension began to mount while they were in the company of this "exceedingly pretty film starlet called Ola" of the company in San Francisco. It seems that she took quite a fancy to Richard's young son. Mr. Lee became edgy and shot warning looks, but things did not reach a head until another exceedingly pretty young woman called June came onto the scene. There came a sudden outburst: "Hands off, she's my wife!" Soon afterwards, Richard blurted out that he was Charles's long-lost father in quite a clumsy manner.

Young Charles was stunned. He said nothing for a while. He later told me that this was a situation where he didn't know what to do with himself. Then it dawned on him as all the rotten images of his childhood came into play: Thackeray College, Battersea, Edmonton; the cold, hunger, the wicked beatings, the education that had been denied to himself and his intelligent sister. "Bigamist!" he shouted and took a swing at him.

In a scene from a film it would happen on the dance floor. They would brawl, the music would stop and everyone would shrink back to the periphery. There would be 'Ohs' and 'Ahs' as the pair packed their punches, the stridency of a police whistle followed by an invasion by the cops . . .

But this was not a film. I neither know details of the location nor who floored who. I imagine that after the scuffle there was silence for a while. Richard had at last framed the words that his son had been semi-expecting. Charles hotly condemned his father for all the hardships he had caused. There followed predictable explanations from Richard. He knew he had been wrong . . . After all he was only young . . . The time was never right . . . Sure as hell the war didn't help . . . He had to live the best he could . . . He had fallen in love again . . . He hadn't meant to cause any pain . . . He sure was a natural-born roamer . . .

It was now, with head hung, that Richard listened as his son told him about the suffering and chaos that had been caused – both to his wife and two children.

I know how dreadful my father felt about the whole situation between his parents and the new 'wife' June. It seems that he kept a lot under his hat when he wrote to his sister on his return from America. Perhaps his light-hearted letter was designed to put his mother off the scent. However, he seems to have taken to June. It is worth remembering that Charles was only eighteen at the time, but I wonder what Marguerite's emotions were if and when she read the letter. Perhaps she read between the lines, or perhaps she already knew. Verses written as she neared old-age suggest that she did. Anyway, the letter is an interesting sketch of life during the Jazz Age:

Gee but you see some creations in Frisco! If I were to launch out on the demerits of female apparel out there, this letter would never be finished, although I only refer to exceptions. In the main, they dress pretty well – Which reminds me, you wanted to know my opinion of the American charmers didn't you? Well of course I wasn't there long enough to form any really definite criticism, and only met two to engage in active conversation. It was hard to form an idea from them as they are different in every way as the two poles so to speak, and although the comparison doesn't appear very vivid – Ola is very flighty and pally – the sort who would go for a country walk with you, fall in a duck pond, and say it was the best afternoon she had ever had! Who calls all sentiment rot, who likes plenty of amusement and good grub, who would love you one moment and jilt you the next, then come back and love you again – Something like Hula Lou, "the sorta gall who never could be true". In short, a proper modern flapper, and as they would say out here, "Doggone good looking!" She rang me up and whispered sweet farewells just before I left and spouted the good old sob stuff over the phone. "Heart Broken Rose." Mash, you know I'd bet my last boot button she was having a rare time with some chap or other an hour or so after! June is just the opposite, not soft and silly you understand, but somehow more steady and reliable, and more the "I'll be ever true," sort. I shan't go on like this or you'll be thinking I'm love-sick Mike or something . . .

It was a poignant mention of June. Marguerite may have given up hope of being reunited with Richard now, but she had not given up her love for him. Charles had made up his mind not to disclose his father's bigamy, but at some point I feel certain that Richard wrote that there was someone else. If June was the "I'll ever be true sort," it is clear that she had plenty in common with Marguerite. Her son had not realised the significance of his words.

That night it was very hot and Charles could not sleep. So much had happened that day. It had been an emotional shock. He kept churning over the situation in his mind. By being in San Francisco he felt disloyal to his mother, yet it was she who had arranged it all. Why, he wondered? Maybe she did so intending that the meeting would be cathartic, that it would draw a line underneath the past once and for all. I have further considered the possibility that, in the knowledge of another woman, she wanted to claim back something of her husband by proxy, through his direct contact with their son. At eighteen-years-old, I doubt that Charles considered the many psychological twists and turns of this unusual situation. On the other hand, maybe his mother was simply being magnanimous. We will never know what entered her mind when she learned that *Scalaria* was destined for America, a mile or two from her beloved Richard.

During the night, as Charles lay there chewing things over in a sweat, he heard a shot. It was followed by another and another. He went to the window that looked into the street and saw a gun-fight. "Just like a cowboy film," he recalled all those years later, "Men scrambling about and hiding from each other, then taking pot-shots." He supposed that it was something to do with gangsters and bootlegging. It certainly helped to establish the ethos – bang in the middle of prohibition America. Richard had not been on the scene. Whether or not he carried a gun nowadays was another matter.

The next day, Richard had to take Charles further down the coast to rejoin the *Scalaria*: "Things were rather quiet as we motored along, but I enjoyed the peace and the scenery. God only knows what was going on in my mind." They stopped for a soft drink before they parted. The conversation turned to Marguerite.

"You know you mother worries about you when you're overseas."

"That's rich. What the devil has it to do with you, anyway?"

"Yeah, you're right."

"Actually, I have thought very seriously about whether I want to become an officer."

"You have?"

"It's a tremendous commitment. It's just that – I'm rather torn. It's my writing. I just can't concentrate on one thing or the other. When I'm on duty – on watch – I find that I'm watching the stars."

"Yeah, you're your mother's son alright. Look, if you wanted to join the naval academy over here I could arrange things for you . . ."

"What?"

"Come to the States."

"After all you've done? You've got a ruddy nerve! Leave mother – after all you put her through?"

"I gotta go on apologising? I hold my hands up."

"I should jolly well think so, you've been a cad. What's the matter, why the smile?"

"You sure sound like your Uncle Arthur, all that public school baloney."

"My Uncle Arthur was the nearest thing I ever had to a father. My father was dead to me. You remember? Look, let's not argue about this. I shall be back home in a few weeks time. What the hell do I tell Mother?"

Perhaps Richard reminisced here a while. Then came the words: "She sure as hell was a good looker. You know, I have very fond memories of Marguerite – your mother. But it sure was a long time ago."

Looking back at his treatment of his wife, it is difficult to suppose that Richard had ever been fond. Marguerite still loved her "wayfaring" husband, and fondness from him in compensation would have hurt her deeply. No doubt his words were designed as a sop to their son.

Before they parted, Richard handed Charles the ring that he always wore on his right finger. Charles accepted it and put it on. He was to wear it until he died. Then Richard clutched at his long-lost son, patted him on the back and drove off. Charles watched the Tin Lizzy wind away into the distance until it was out of sight, turned and went up the gang plank, once again putting the distance of an ocean between them.

Passing

For a while after her brother's meeting with their father, Phyllis sent some of her children's stories to Richard. Both children corresponded with him for a while after that, but communication eventually petered out, until . . .

In 1936, while Charles was living as a recluse working the land, writing poetry, and submitting paragraphs for *Punch*, a startling letter arrived from June. Richard was dead. But how was he to tell his mother? His father's name had not been mentioned for many years, albeit that Marguerite still held his letters close.

I imagine my grandmother as she swept up the letter from the mat, hoping for the latest news or publication from her son. Instead she read the letter that marked the end of a protracted dream: Richard was dead! Dick was gone! It is sad to visualise how she must have cried; for the days when they were young in the heat of an Edwardian summer; for the memory of when he waved goodbye at the corner and was lost to her; for the children who would always remain, in her mind, their sleeping babies; and for a past of fading hopes and the lost years in between.

Marguerite found solace in nature in later years: "Wherever the bluebell rings its call, it is Sunday in the woods and in your heart," she wrote at about that time. I do

Charles Ackerman Berry in the early 1930s as a writer for Punch

not think that it stretches the imagination to see her walking along a craggy headland in Cornwall, the breeze gently blowing her wispy grey hair. She looks far out to sea at the horizon, a horizon like the one in her mind that used to call her to Richard – no matter where she was or what she was doing. Perhaps she composed her poem on that headland. I do know that after she received the news she sat down and wrote the following lyric, re-establishing her love for her errant husband:

I do not Grieve

I do not grieve
That summer days are ended!
I cannot wish
Our love had never been!
I cannot hope
That broken hearts be mended;
Nor can my soul
A ray of comfort glean.

I had my hour
When life was full of sunshine.
You loved me then,
And I? I worshipped you!
You went away!
The love I though was all mine
Another stole,
I often wonder who.

But there remains
A memory that's hidden
Deep in my heart,
Where none may gaze or pry.
I do not grieve,
I loved you all unbidden!
I only know
I'll love you till I die.

In 1967, my grandmother was staying in a Devon nursing home with Dorothy, when a serious fire broke out. In the chaos, she tried to dash back into the flames to rescue Dorothy and had to be restrained. She soon saw that Dorothy was safe, but grew agitated: the letters tied up in a blue ribbon that she had kept safe for so long - letters from Richard – perished. She had nothing to hold close now.

Marguerite Ackerman Berry died in 1969 at the age of eighty three cared for by nuns. I was a nurse working in a hospital across the road at the time. I did not know her story then, yet somehow I sensed great sadness about her life. I held her hand as she lay there breathing stertorously, the tears coursing down my cheeks. A little while later, my father told me that he dreamed about his mother in a meadow. She appeared serene and content, sitting underneath a beautiful tree. She told him how nice it was to see him and added: "I know everything now." Everything? Could that mean Richard's secrets, or some of the great mysteries of life and death which we grasp in a moment and lose hold of?

The Web of Time

Some years later, after I read my grandmother's poem, I was deeply saddened. Over and over again the same question arose: "Why did he hurt her, why?" Soon afterwards, in a mystical half-dream between sleeping and waking, I found myself inside the Theatre Royal, Haymarket, during the Edwardian era. I glided lightly from the back of the auditorium, through a glass door marked 'teas' and observed. It seems strange now, for although the people were talking and clinking their spoons against their cups, I was not conscious of the sound. I glided through the door back into the auditorium and floated from the aisle to the stage. I stood on the stage and looked out over the footlights to a haze, turned and lightly followed my destined course behind the great curtain. Then I rose up and into the narrow corridors that housed the dressing rooms. I have often wondered whether I passed like a wisp through John Buckstone as I trespassed among his haunts, but I held fast to my purpose. Somewhere nearby along another narrow corridor was an office, and I glided through the door. A young man was standing behind a desk. It was Richard.

"Why did you hurt her, why?" I asked him. He seemed startled, but did not answer. Then I awoke.

The Refreshment Department
is under the direct control of
THE MANAGEMENT

All spirits, wines, beers and minerals
are well-known brands of the best
quality, and are sold at ordinary
Café charges.

◇ ◇

1/- AFTERNOON TEAS 1/-

A Special Service of Afternoon Tea, freshly
made for each order, with pastry, cake and
bread and butter, is served at Matinées in the
Auditorium and Saloons.
Orders in advance greatly facilitate service.

◇ ◇

CHOCOLATES

Dainty plain and fancy chocolates by
Nestlé, Caller, and Warren & Co. are
on sale at Shop Prices from One Shilling
per box.

◇ ◇

COFFEE
6d. · Specially made every Evening · 6d.

◇ ◇

6d. · LEMON SQUASH · 6d.
Made with Hooper Struve's Lemonade and Rose's Lemon Juice.

From the Haymarket Theatre

Again, it would be easy to say, "Only a dream", but I soon found that this was different. To date, I had never been inside the Haymarket Theatre, but when I described the interior to my father, he assured me that, many years ago, there was a tea room at the back just as I had described. "Arthur used to bring back éclairs from the same tea room when I was a young boy. I don't know about an office, though," he said. I wrote to tell Aunt Phyllis, who sent a page from an old theatre programme by return of post. It was an advertisement for the tea room. A little later, she sent me a silver spoon engraved: Theatre Royal, Haymarket. It became clear to all of us that I had somehow explored the territory in my dream. I was excited, but kept an open mind. Nonetheless, I determined to see the place for myself and wrote to the Haymarket, but I was refused permission. I was undeterred and immediately wrote to Ingrid Bergman who was appearing in *Waters of the Moon*. I explained my dream and asked whether she could help me to gain access to the theatre. A week or so later, a signed photograph by way of recognition came through the post. It was followed by a letter from her stage manager. Arrangements were made and very soon I was off to the Haymarket, although several weeks later I began to have doubts about my 'psychic' experience.

But the doubts did not last long. I began my tour from the back of the theatre and was at once jolted into recognition. Everything was strangely familiar. I approached the tea shop and saw that it was now a bar, but 'Teas' was still clearly visibly written on the glass door. The stage manager shot a querying look as we passed along the aisle and onto the stage. Perhaps it was in response to something that he saw in my own expression. I vaguely remember him mentioning the resident ghost, but I paid no heed and climbed up onto the stage.

I stood on the set of *Waters of the Moon* and felt wrapped in a blue haze which went out beyond the footlights and into the auditorium. Everything was a mirror image of my dream, except the revolving set with its ornamented mantelpiece, period furniture and dummy piano. I could have stayed there forever, but was prompted to follow on behind the stage manager. He pulled back the heavy curtain to reveal a tangle of rope – some wound haphazardly around cleats, and I looked up at the sheer drop from the flies. The *déjà vu* was still evident, and, unafraid, I continued along a known path. Somehow we arrived at a flight of steps, and it was then that I began to describe the rooms ahead of me.

"There's a narrow corridor ahead," I said. The stage manager nodded. Once into the corridor that housed the dressing rooms, I described a similar space above. The stage manager was intrigued. Surely, he thought, I had been there before. I assured him that I had not – in usual circumstances, that is. I followed my leader up more stairs and I was able to describe the position of the doors before we approached. One was the same door which had led to Richard's office. I did not go in, but, reluctantly, finished the round trip and swung back into the sunlight.

The fact that I had proved my experience – I had actually been to the Haymarket Theatre in my dreams – led me to suppose that, all else being so, I had seen, really seen, Richard. A host of questions demanded an answer. What was Richard doing in the office at that time? Was he working there, or was he an interloper? Marguerite recorded that he was "in serious trouble" before he left the country. Perhaps it was the scene of a crime as Wynne Ackerman once hinted. My great grandmother, Anne Ackerman, worked at the Haymarket for a few years after she fell on hard times. Moreover, her son Arthur had performed in the same theatre. My enquiries at the Haymarket yielded nothing, and Richard, at that time, remained as elusive as ever.

But even more intriguing questions arise. Did Richard see me, his granddaughter, like a ghost? Did he narrow his eyes to discern a form and the vague outline of a spectral future? Perhaps he heard a sound at the door and shuddered at the thought of old Buckstone exercising his ghostly squatter's rights? Or was I, a wraith of my dreams, invisible to his physical eyes? I cannot answer these questions, but can relate what happened at the Haymarket Theatre – seemingly before I was actually born.

As for the intriguing story, questions about what could have happened or what would have happened surfaced again and again as I dipped into memoirs and vague recollections of the past, and I often found a feast of possibilities. I cannot explain how or why I have been haunted by my grandmother's story with its portrait of the husband who had caused so much pain over a hundred years ago. But it would be unjust to cast Richard as a villain, knowing so little about the hidden episodes of his life. After all, the antics of Richard Percy Berry (alias Richard Lee) are recorded in the Book of Time – and with Charlie Chaplin on celluloid.

Today, I often re-live the day that as a fifteen-year-old girl in pigtails, I entered that little cottage on the edge of a Cornish moor and found pictures of Richard and Marguerite when they were young and full of hope. Perhaps it was intended that I should. And as I picked up her pen in later years: "like all dreamers, I was possessed on a sudden with supernatural powers and passed like a spirit through the barrier before me . . ."[16]

---

[16] From Daphne du Maurier's *Rebecca*.